FATHER GREELEY was [born in Oak] Park, Illinois, in 1928. He attended Quigley Preparatory Seminary and studied philosophy and theology at St. Mary of the Lake Seminary at Mundelein. He has been a curate at Christ the King Church in Chicago since his ordination and served as editor of *The Apostolate*. He received his doctorate in sociology from the University of Chicago in 1962, and continues research at the National Opinion Research Center there. Father Greeley has written for numerous magazines, among them *America, Commonweal, The Critic, The Sign,* and *Ave Maria,* and is the author of *The Church in the Suburbs, Strangers in the House, Religion and Career* and *And Young Men Shall See Visions.*

Letters to Nancy

Letters to Nancy

FROM
Andrew M. Greeley

SHEED AND WARD : NEW YORK

Manufactured in the United States of America

For Nancy and all the others like her

Preface

It is with some considerable risk that a male, especially a celibate male, presumes to offer advice to women of any age. He can be readily dismissed as not knowing anything about the situation—or worse. Indeed, when the article that preceded this volume first appeared in *Ave Maria,* at least one member of the parish to which I am assigned expressed curiosity as to why I hated women. I was somewhat taken aback by this accusation, but then if I could have understood what it meant, perhaps I would not have been so foolhardy to write the article in the first place.

Like its companion volume* this one is not an attempt to develop a systematic or theologically elegant treatise on the spiritual life. It rather represents in highly concrete fashion the approach used at one place at one time. This particular approach cannot claim even to be as successful as was the one recorded in the companion volume—which is pretty unsuccessful indeed. At best, I suppose, it is a footnote in the history of the contemporary attempts to develop a spirituality for young lay people.

* *And Young Men Shall See Visions* (New York, Sheed & Ward, 1963).

Whatever my covert ambivalences towards womankind, I must thank a good number of them for keeping more major errors out of this work: Helen Calteaux, Grace Ann Carroll, Sister Brigid, C.S.J., Fran Norris, Sue Durburg, and Mary Jule Durkin, the last mentioned of whom is apparently fated to go through life having to defend the crazy things her brother writes. In this particular volume at least neither she nor any of the others are to be held culpable.

We must also express our gratitude to the Reverend John F. Hotchkin, whose ideas have been shamelessly stolen. And finally we must thank "Nancy" for listening.

Andrew M. Greeley

Contents

Letters to Nancy

An Invitation

Dear Nancy,

If you asked me—and I know you haven't—what the most important virtue is for a girl your age, I think I should reply that the required virtue is fidelity. In the ordinary usage this virtue is taken to have to do with the loyalty of a woman to her husband or to the man she loves, the kind of loyalty so beautifully described in Manzoni's *The Betrothed* (which I have a hunch you never did get through). However, this usage is really a restriction to one area of life of a virtue which has a much broader application. The kind of fidelity I have in mind is fidelity to an ideal, to a vision of what life is all about, to the higher impulses of human nature, to one's own better self.

I remember that we once had a conversation about "reverse hypocrisy"—that peculiar tendency of modern young people to want to appear less good than they really are. We noted that the person whom we were discussing—charitably I hope—was afraid to admit to himself how good he actually was, perhaps because of the obligations that would follow from such an admission; so he was often content to pretend

3

that he was ordinary and something less than ordinary. Reverse hypocrisy is the vice opposed to the virtue of fidelity and it is a vice which rather effectively destroys fidelity. It seems to me that this kind of infidelity is the worst temptation that young people your age must face, and that it is especially severe for girls.

In one sense, Nancy, the Vision a girl your age will have is much more noble than that of a boy. His Vision will be of himself doing great things. Hers will rather be of herself manifesting great love. He sees things to be done; she sees people to be cared for. He wants to bring more of the rationality of the divine order into the world; she wants to make the world a warmer place by offering it God's love. In the face of physical suffering, a boy feels very awkward and embarrassed. He is angered by what he sees, but he does not know what to do; a girl, on the other hand, knows exactly how to bring tenderness into the lives of those who desperately need it. Surely you will have noticed this in the apostolic work your group has done in past years.

There is no one more generous or more sensitive to human suffering than an adolescent girl; this is one of the reasons, I suppose, why girls are objectively so much more attractive to adults than their bumbling male counterparts. Indeed, their generosity may often be erratic and superficial and occasionally even imprudent, yet there is so little genuine emotional warmth in the world that one hates to see this youthful flame put out. When a boy is unfaithful to his Vision, the world loses a bit of vigor and order; when a girl is unfaithful to hers, the world loses a bit of love. I think there is a strong human tendency to say, "the order we can do without, the love we cannot."

When we aging types watch such a girl at work in the first flush of her generous affection for everyone (and everything) in sight, we are tempted to say, "Ah, if she could only stay that way; if she could only balance her generosity with maturity and prudence and depth, then she would really be someone; she would be the kind of woman who would be irresistible. There would be nothing she could not do." But, alas, it does not last very long. Shortly the fire seems to turn to ice. And if there is nothing more attractive, Nancy, than a generous young woman, there is nothing more repelling than a selfish old woman, especially when she is selfish and old at twenty-two.

What is the Vision to which a young girl can be unfaithful? Imagine that you were born blind and that for sixteen or seventeen years you could see nothing. Then suddenly one day you were able to see. What a glorious and splendid place the world would seem—full of color and motion, light and shadow, the marvelous and the fearsome. In the first few months and years after you had begun to see, the world would have been new and fresh and exciting, and you would have wanted to see everything in it and come to know and love as much as you could of its beauty. But then, as time passed, the newness would wear off, the splendor would fade, the lights would grow dim, and the world would be for you what it is for those who had their sight from childhood—dull, drab, and commonplace.

It seems to me that everyone in their late teens goes

through an emotional and psychological experience something like this. The child and the early adolescent is a remarkably unperceptive creature. He takes the world and himself for granted, much as he does the air he breathes. It is neither good nor bad, interesting or dull, but simply unnoticed. Then there comes the awakening; amidst a considerable amount of stress and confusion, the young person discovers the world and discovers himself as mirrored in the world. The reaction is the same as that of the blind person I described in the last paragraph. The world is thrilling, exciting, challenging, fascinating. All the unspoiled vigor and generosity and enthusiasm of youth is poured forth in a torrent of energy. The world is good, but it must be made better. There is suffering and it must be brought to an end. Mankind is going in the wrong direction and must be turned around and be pointed the right way. Life is just beginning, the decades stretch ahead full of promise, there is much to be seen, much to be done, much to be loved. The young person looks around, notices how dull and uninteresting and unproductive are the lives of many adults, and he resolves that this will not happen to him. He has but one life and he is going to do something with it. When he is finished the world is going to be a better place for his having lived. He is going to give the human race a good strong shove and heaven help the human race if it tries to fight back. The poor, the sick, the lonely, he is going to help; the unloved he is going to love; the ignorant he is going to instruct, the tyrannical he is going to dethrone, the old-fashioned he is going to put in their place. Of such is the stuff of revolutions and inventions, of

great art and poetry, of prophecy and sanctity. But alas, it
is not to be. For just as the person who has been physically
blind gradually grows accustomed to the world he has discovered, so the emerging adult finds the bright glare which
youthful vision has revealed to be too brilliant, and he turns
away from it, back to the blindness of early adolescence. He
has become an adult, or rather he has become middle-aged
at twenty-one.

For the Christian the discovery-experience is more
dazzling and hence the ultimate infidelity is much worse.
The young Christian discovers not only his fellowmen; he
(or she) also discovers that mighty reality which underlies
the unity of the human race and will ultimately perfect it—
the Mystical Body. In one awesome instant it dawns on the
young person that all the formulae he has memorized in
school are in a very different category from stories about
Santa Claus and the elves. Christ really did come into the
world to straighten out the mess mankind had got into. He
really did die on the Cross for all of us; He really did rise
from the dead; the Church really continues His work in the
world, and we are all really part of this great endeavor on
which the future of mankind depends. For a few moments
at least, the young person realizes with terrible clarity that
he is part of the Church, indeed, in the words of Pius XII,
he *is* the Church. It is at this time that thought about religious vocations begins, sometimes because God has really
planted the seed of a vocation, more often because even in
this "age of the laity," young people have picked up the
impression that only the clergy or the religious can be part

of the work of the Church. It is also at this time that the
desire to renounce the world becomes strong, because it so
often seems that Christ can be found only by isolating ourselves from our fellowmen, that the world is too confused
and corrupt for us to survive in and that therefore the best
thing to do is to flee it. The young person yearns to get away
from it all, from the stupidity, the trivia, the nonsense that
seem so large a part of human life. It is only in quiet and
solitude that one can pray and it is only in the prayer of
quiet that God can be found.

Such an attitude is a betrayal of the prior human
insight about the splendor of the world and the need that
it be made more splendid. It assumes that man sees the
world as a marvelous and reformable place, and then the
Christian sees it as corrupted by sin and beyond reform. We
know that grace does not destroy nature and so if a seem-
ingly Christian insight is contrary to a valid natural insight
—then it is not really Christian. The Calvinist may have
despaired of the world; the Catholic has not. He knows that
the whole of material creation, the whole of human society,
the magnificent complex of human organization, human art,
human technology, has been redeemed. Christ rose from the
dead to bring life not just to the soul but to the whole human
person, body included. And through the human body the
grace of Christ's Resurrection flows to the rest of creation.
It is through our lives and our work that the Gospel is
brought to our fellowmen and the saving imprint of sancti-
fied human reason is impressed on the rest of creation. We
do not find Christ merely in the quiet of contemplation; we

find Him in the least of the brothers whom we feed or instruct, we find Him in our work, we find Him everywhere. And eventually everything will be united to Him through us and to God through Him; the work of the Resurrection will be complete, and we will have been part of it.

God does not deflect our gaze prematurely from the work He Himself has given us, since He presents Himself to us as attainable through that very work. Nor does He blot out, in His intense light, the detail of our earthly aims, since the intimacy of our union with Him is in fact a function of the exact fulfillment of the least of our tasks. . . . God in all that is most living and incarnate in Him, is not withdrawn from us beyond the tangible sphere; He is waiting for us at every moment in our action, in our work of the moment. He is in some sort at the tip of my pen, my spade, my brush, my needle, of my heart and my thought. By pressing the stroke, the line, or the stitch, on which I am engaged, to its ultimate natural finish, I shall arrive at the ultimate aim towards which my innermost will trends.*

Now I should think that this is a pretty exciting Vision; in fact, the trouble with it is that it seems almost too good to be true. We find it very difficult to believe that we can be part of something so great. And so in our more sober moments we look back on the Vision and dismiss it as a daydream. For the priest, the religious, the contemplative such things may be possible, but for the mundane, struggling layman they cannot be.

I have nothing against the contemplative vocation. It is

* P. Teilhard de Chardin, *The Divine Milieu* (New York: Harper, 1960), pp. 33-34.

surely a noble life, the most noble to which man can be called. But is it not an escape from the world? He who runs to La Trappe to escape from the world will very shortly return, because reality is much more evident in a monastery than in the world. The contemplative leaves the world because he loves it so much that he wishes to dedicate his whole life to praying for it. If he does not, he will not be a contemplative very long.

However, it is of the essence of Christianity to believe that the work of the Church is the work of every Christian, so much so that St. Thomas can speak of the Sacrament of Baptism as a quasi-ordination. When you were baptized, Nancy, you were consecrated to the work of the Church; you were dedicated to representing Christ in the world, to bringing His truth to the ignorant, His light to the confused, His love to the lonely; the seal of the sacrament marked you as one whose life was to be devoted to promoting the reign of God-guided human reason over the irrationality that abounds in the world. It was to be the task of your life and your work to push back the darkness of sin and error and misery until they are finally banished from the earth. Ordination or religious profession only specify certain areas in which one is to work. It is Baptism and Confirmation that mark you irrevocably as a co-worker of the Resurrection—the bringing of life to the world.

This vocation is yours and that of thousands of young men and women your age. Only a few of you will be called to pursue it in a monastery or a rectory or a convent, but the rest of you can not escape its demands except by paying a heavy price. You may try to excuse your infidelity to such a vision of life by saying that it is too great and wonderful to be true, but all you succeed in doing when you argue in this fashion is to show how weak your faith is.

I could never understand why young people are so hesitant to believe that the Vision is more real than the everyday reality in which they are immersed. Surely it demands sacrifices of them, surely it demands that they put off the phoniness of reverse hypocrisy, surely it demands that they must live with doubt and uncertainty, that they will be called fools or laughed at. But it should seem to me that in the excitement of being young the splendor of the Christian vision ought to provide a way out for those who do not want to be mediocre. At the very time when the young person is faced with the overwhelming question of what he is to do with his life, the Christian vision provides a dynamic answer; yet the answer is so often rejected—and for what seem to be the poorest of reasons.

Part of the reason for the rejection is that young people really don't have the right idea of what Christianity is all about. You ask someone what the purpose of life is and he will parrot back, "to know, love and serve God in this world so as to save my soul in this life and be happy with Him in the next." This is not necessarily a false answer, but it admits of false interpretations. Cardinal Suenens of Belgium has recently rephrased the answer in a marvelous fashion, "To know God and bring others to know him, to love God and to bring others to love him, and to serve God and lead others to his service." He might well have added, "and so to share in the work of bringing life to the world and thus be happy both in this life and in the next." We are not running away from the world, Nancy, we're going to change it. We are not going to hide in our secure little ghetto and let the rest of the world go on its merry way to damnation. I read recently of a girl working as a medical missionary in South Vietnam; a newspaper man asked her whether she had any vows that were part of this vocation. Her reply was right to the point, "Yes, my baptismal vows!" You don't need anything else, Nance, to have a vocation, and if you ignore the implications of these vows in your daily life, you are going to cheat yourself out of an extraordinarily exciting life.

Well, this is really an awful way to start a correspondence with a girl who is just beginning her college adventures. I promise that I will try to be less grim in the future. We are in the process of trying to reorganize the YCS around here; the casualties have been high in the moderator group with everyone going off to college. However, we have some good prospects and we might be able to salvage the organization. We'll keep you posted.

God bless,

Life Is for Living

Dear Nancy,

If I am to believe the papers, you already have snow out in the Rockies; this will teach you to leave Chicago for such desolate regions. After all, you see mountains once, what's left about them that is exciting? As for skiing, I am convinced that it is immoral, but I don't seem to be able to persuade anyone else of this. Only don't expect any sympathy when you end up in a hospital in Denver with a broken leg.

I'm glad you liked the redefinition by Cardinal Suenens of the purpose of the Christian life; you are quite correct when you say that it is unfortunate that this emphasis is not to be found in much of Catholic education. However, take heart; when your children are entering first grade (in about fifteen years I presume), the so-called new approach (which is really very old) will be much more common than it is today. One of the difficulties with your generation, Nance, and I guess with all young people (sure sign of old age), is that when you see that something ought to be changed you want the change to take place before eight o'clock the next morning. For all kinds of reasons, the catechetical approach of the Church has been pretty much frozen since the Council of Trent. The Church was so beleaguered, so much on the defensive, that there did not seem to be any opportunity to work for more profound understanding of what the truths of the faith could mean in the life of a layman. We thought really that we were lucky just to keep the laity in the Church and were not in a position (or at least thought we were not) to develop any theology of the laity or theology for the laity. Hence, the old answers of the catechism had to serve. But towards the end of the last century, almost without anyone knowing it, things began to change; the revivals in liturgy, scripture, catechetics, and theology begin to have an ever-larger influence on the life of the Church. The Second Vatican Council, from one point of view, is simply a method for consolidating the gains.

All of this means that when parents say, "Well, I never heard of that before" about something you may have picked up in theology class or a YCS moderators' meeting, they are telling the exact truth; they never did hear of it. They grew up in a different world, even though it was only a few years ago; they went to school during the world of the Counter-Reformation and you are going to school at the beginning of a new world, one which, for the lack of a better name, we are now calling the Ecumenic Age—or, perhaps even better, the Age of Pope John.

An outstanding example of the effect of this change on our understanding of the meaning of our faith is the subject of grace. We learned in grammar school (though kids are learning differently today) that it is a "supernatural gift of God"—an answer that you will still get from most college people if you catch them off guard with a question about "what is grace?" Now this answer isn't wrong, but it doesn't tell half, no, not even a hundredth, of the story. As one modern writer describes it, grace is much more than just a gift:

Grace unites God and man, more exactly, grace is God's way of meeting man whom he came in search of and found lost in the solitude of an earthly sinful nature. In this meeting, God's love takes to itself man as he is, the whole of him, and makes of him a child of the Father, with and in the only begotten Son, through the power of the Holy Spirit. Grace is the marvelous point of contact between the two worlds: the world of the triune infinitude and that of the utter nothingness which is man.*

Quite clearly this is something much more than the absence of mortal sin. Grace is not merely a state, a static condition which marks us off from those who "don't have it"; it is, rather, the secret of God's presence in our life; it is the vital energy of the Divinity giving force and direction to our existence. It is not some vague ethereal quality that would make us acceptable if we should present ourselves at the entrance to heaven on the morrow. It is rather

God's creative, loving way of speaking to each one of us individually in Christ and in the Church. . . . The divine word does not find us located in the rarefied regions of a stratospheric spiritual-

---

* Peter Fransens, S.J., *Divine Grace and Man* (New York: Desclee, 1962), p. 67.

ity where the trifling care and responsibilities of the puny world are lost to sight. God speaks to us in the very concrete situation which is ours. The essential message of the Redemption and grace is that we must surrender ourselves to God in faith, hope and charity, *here and now* on this earth, in the spot to which Providence has consigned us and in which He wills us to dwell.*

You can see how this idea of grace fits in with the ideas about the Resurrection we heard from Fr. H. during the summer. Christ came into the world to bring us Life when we were dead with the death of sin, life not just to the spiritual element but to the whole man, body and soul. The Resurrection represents His victory over sin and death. Grace is life, the continuation of the Resurrection, the promise of future physical resurrection, at work in the life of each Christian and in the life of the Whole Christ which is His Church. If we think of grace this way we realize that it is not merely a state, but an energy, not something with merely spiritual effects, but also with profoundly physical results, not indeed a thing but a Person operating in harmony with our personality, not just a Life in the next world, but a Life in this one too.

But it is not enough that we be in loving contact with this Personality which is transforming our own personality. We must bear witness to this Personality in the world around us so that all things will be "transformed in Him."

Christian humanism is not entrusted only with the negative role of clearing external obstacles out of the way of grace, or with the

* *Ibid.*, p. 12.

mere task of serving the Church in her apostolate. It should take
pride in the profound positive and religious vocation received in
and through grace. God's word makes the world transparent,
turns it into a shrine and tabernacle of the divine living presence.
More still, all goodness, truth, virtue and beauty, concealed in
the world, has been given to us in commission. Our humble obe-
dience to grace which is the secret of our salvation, demands that
we take it all in hand, use it, cause it to bloom. A Catholic doctor
finds in his faith a deeper, more convincing motive for a competent practice of his profession; so also the poet, the engineer, the
social worker, the laborer or farmer. To put it in other words: our
earthly career does not lie outside our Christian calling, but, on
the contrary, well within it. Or more correctly still: our deep
fundamental self-surrender to God in faith and charity has to find
expression in the concrete details of our earthly career and dedication. On this level too we are God's fellow workers. The world
is to us a 'divine milieu' in which our earthly life achieves, thanks
to God's love, its fullest meaning.*

No more long quotations, Nance, but that one says
everything so beautifully. Grace is a dynamic energy in our
life, it is God calling on us to be as thoroughly human as we
can possibly be, because the more human we are the better
we reflect the glory of His Presence. It is God urging us not
to hide our light under a bushel, but rather to let His light
flow on the mountain top. We have come a long way from
the "supernatural gift of God" idea and a much longer way
from the "absence of mortal sin" mentality.

I suppose we could say that grace is the Vision seen
from the inside; it is the reality within the Vision and the

* *Ibid.*, p. 108.

force which will sustain the Vision through difficulties and obstacles—if we give it a chance. Grace, Life, Vision—they are all the same thing looked at from slightly different perspective.

One of the real agonies of our job, Nance, is that we see so many young people, filled with the vigor of fresh human life, who permit that life to grow stale and hard because they are willing to settle for phoney life. They do not realize that grace sustains and perfects life. They are afraid that they must choose between human life and grace, between the joys and happiness they want out of human existence and the demands of their religion. They do not realize that grace will not destroy human life, nor deprive it of its joys, but rather make it wider and deeper and more rewarding. I get the impression that people are often running from us because they are afraid that we will demand that they relinquish their life, while in reality we only want to offer them more life, more life, indeed, than they would dream possible. As Fr. H. says in his more elfin moments, "we've got to persuade people that being a Christian is fun." Well, if fun means a rich full life, then there is nothing that is more fun than being a Christian. Christ came into the world precisely that we might have a full life, and grace is the divine energy which communicates this full life to each human personality. Only those whose eyes have never been open or have been dimmed by cynicism and disappointment would be so stupid as to pass up the chance.

There are some practical implications of this doctrine of grace as living energy which you might want to ponder.

I think that there is a rather subtle danger that young people at the beginning of life are inclined to think that life still lies in the future. One begins to live only after one is out of college or working in one's career or engaged or raising children. These things are life; all the rest is preliminary and not especially important except as preparation. The unfortunate part of this "tomorrow mentality" is that life will never begin, it will always be something just beyond the next rise in the ground, because the person has never known the meaning of the "sacrament of the present moment." Life is not tomorrow or next year or some future event; it is now, it is in the challenge of the present situation, it is being lonely and a bit confused and away from friends and family and having to study for a distasteful biology exam. It is skiing (despite Father Greeley's warnings) in the foothills of the Rockies; it is writing a letter to a friend; it is putting up with people whose different temperaments disturb you. It is the satisfaction of a challenging lecture or a good article and the taste of a hamburger (no mustard, please). The past is gone, the future may never come. Life is the present, grace operates in the present. I may seem strange to link life with hamburgers, skiing, letter-writing and biology tests. All of these activities seem so mundane and commonplace; but for someone with vision nothing is commonplace, and mundane is an adjective of approval. Life does not consist of external events, important or unimportant, but rather of our orientation towards these events. If you cannot find joy and excitement and challenge in what you are doing now, then you will never find these characteristics of life any-

where. If the reality of grace does not transform your existence when you are a sophomore in college, it never will
(unless, of course, you drastically alter your orientation).

I should think that these are rather terrifying words,
Nance. To put it as bluntly as possible: if you cannot find
happiness in college when you have everything going for
you, I don't see how—short of a miracle of God's help—you
ever will. If serenity and joy are not characteristic of you
when you have the strength and beauty of youth, there's no
reason to think that they are going to come later on. If you
are not alive now, you never will be alive. If you have become the emotional and spiritual equivalent of a corpse at
nineteen, you are not going to rise again at thirty-nine (and
you will be that age some day, even though that hardly
seems possible now). If your life is narrow and anxious and
stunted and distraught now, it will hardly improve with the
years. All of which is to say that if grace has not begun to
animate your existence now, the beginning is going to be
increasingly difficult as the years go on. If your Vision has
begun to fade now, it will be invisible before you are thirty.

God has been very good to you, Nancy; He has given
you a tremendous amount of natural vigor and vitality. The
structure of your personality is such that it is wide open to
the operation of grace. There are no (or very few) natural
obstacles to the transformation of your life in Christ Jesus
(as St. Paul puts it). This is a great advantage but it is also
a harsh responsibility. Whatever obstacles block the operation of grace in your personality will be those that you have
put there with your own free will, either through ignorance

or malice, or maybe only fear. If you blow the chances you have now, if you waste the precious few years of college, then you may never get another chance.

It would not be at all unusual for someone your age and of your temperament to have emotional ups and downs; this is not what I have in mind. But if you find yourself consistently anxious and troubled, then there is obviously something wrong, you are putting some kind of obstacle in the way of the work of grace. Find out what that obstacle is and get rid of it. God made us to be happy and if we are unhappy it is because we are resisting grace—probably in many instances without being quite sure explicitly what we are doing wrong.

I hope it is clear that I am not identifying happiness or peace with the absence of suffering. A person with vision, a person who is aware of what grace means in his life, can be under great physical or emotional suffering—at the time of sickness or when a loved one dies—and still not lose the basic orientation of faith which brings peace to his life. I am not saying grace removes suffering, but I am saying that in the reasonably stable person it ought to furnish a profound peace, a sense of direction and mission which can co-exist with all kinds of external difficulties and cares. If this sense that your life is going in the right direction, a direction you have chosen, is present most of the time, then I don't think you should have any fears that you are resisting the operation of grace. If this sense of direction is absent or if some counterfeit has replaced it, then, Nancy, you have troubles and you must move against them quickly. If you are not getting any satisfaction out of your present state of life, the problem is not the state of life but you, and a change in state will not eliminate the problem.

Another conclusion from the theology of grace is that we must seize opportunities. I don't mean that you ought to be a thrill-hunter, but I do mean that you must not pass up obvious opportunities for an enrichment of your life when these opportunities are clearly available. Thus I would not argue that it would be to resist grace not to go to Europe for a year (as John is doing); but it could be in some cases. The Spirit blows where He wills, and if He blows in the direction of a year in Europe or an orchestra concert or a difficult but interesting book by inclining you in the direction of these things, and you resist the inclination because of fear or laziness or lethargy, then it seems to me that you are stunting your life. We must not feel that grace helps us only to have pious thoughts or to resist temptation; it also orients us towards everything that will make us more richly human and more fully Christian. If the new understanding of grace means anything, it means that grace and nature are not opposed but intermingled in the perfection of the Christian personality. When you resist becoming that which you are capable of becoming, you resist grace.

A dreadfully threatening letter, I must admit, Nancy. But I guess it is part of my job to threaten people every once in a while. Give my best to Peg. Our new moderators are showing some promise. We may have found a formula that works.

God bless,

The Lived No

Dear Nancy,

I really didn't want to inject the question of sin into my discussion of resisting grace, but since you raised it, I ought to comment. And to get to the point immediately, I definitely think that when a young person refuses to become himself or herself, he or she is sinning.

Let us think about the story of the rich young man. I know that the popular explanation of this story is that the man had an invitation which he was free to accept or not to accept and that he refused without any guilt. But there is another interpretation (which I am stealing from a wonderful book by a young Jesuit theologian named John Gerken). The rich young man was not satisfied with his life; he was troubled, restless, unhappy. He became aware that Jesus was the kind of man who could put meaning into his life. He asked Jesus what was necessary that he might find peace and happiness. Jesus told him what was required for *him* (though the same thing might not be offered to someone else). The rich young man did not accept. He not only turned his back on Jesus and on the invitation of Jesus; he

23

turned his back on the possibility of happiness and ultimately he turned his back on himself. Father Gerken has
this to say about those who resist a solution to their restlessness:

If the person deliberately suppresses this restlessness, if he tries
to escape it by imposing pseudo obligations, or if he deliberately
hurts himself by making the cause of his disturbance last, then he
sins. If, on the other hand, he decides to fulfill what he knows
conduces to his peace, then as this decision becomes actualized,
there is a sense of completion; his basic attitude of mind, the
principle of his personal being, is thereby strengthened and in its
own goodness and is opened even wider than before to the call
of God. It has had experience, it has acquired the first strains of
a habit of responding to this, and it is thus capable of prompter
and fuller surrender when the next call comes or when the details
of the same call manifest themselves. The person is thus progress-
ing towards greater and greater integrity—his response to God
becomes more total so that it approaches the totality of the demand, 'Love God with your whole heart.'*

That is a lot of perhaps complicated theology, Nancy;
let's put the matter more concretely. When you turn away
from yourself, you are turning away from God, you are
taking out of your life the orientation that God wanted you
to put in it. You are refusing to be yourself. An extremely
interesting aspect of Father Gerken's book is that he thinks
his theory applies just as much to the lay vocation as to the
religious vocation. I suppose that you have heard often about

* From *Toward a Theology of the Layman*, by John D. Gerken, S.J.,
published by Herder and Herder, New York 16. Page 117.

how the religious vocation was a "better" one than the lay vocation. But Father Gerken has this to say,

It is simply false to say that the lay state is adequately explained as the state of those who are not as generous as religious. It is not the state of those who are willing to dally on the road to perfection and who do not want to take the more efficient means to holiness; nor is it the state of those who want to divide their hearts between God and the world. And conversely the religious state is not adequately explained by saying it is the state of the more generous, of those who have given themselves wholly to God.*

From this point of view the vocation of the layman is as important as the vocation of the religious. Father Gerken goes so far as to say that only the mature person can aspire to be a Christian layman in the fullest sense of the word.

The layman's love of God is not indirect but direct. When he loves his family, his society, his work, his country he is directly loving God at the same time. If the indirect way means that one loves creatures when he really could love God without loving the creatures, then such a person does not love God with his whole heart, mind, and strength. And that is forbidden a Christian. If indirect means only that one does not take the vows or undertake a life of prayer . . . but lives God's will for him in the world, then that way is no less direct than the way of the religious or the priest. All seek God's will. That will cannot be anything else but that they love him primarily and directly. When they do not do this, they sin; there is no room for more or less within the first great commandment. Total love of God is demanded of all Chris-

* *Ibid.,* p. 55.

tians. But total renouncement is not demanded of all Christians; therefore total renouncement cannot be conceived of as the only means to total love, and it cannot claim for itself the title of the direct way to God.*

So let us have done with the thought that your present vocation is a second-rate one, that it demands of you less love than a religious vocation would have. There is indeed a sense in which the religious vocation is better, and that is (according to Father Gerken and his teacher, Father Karl Rahner), that it manifests through renunciation the other-worldly aspect of the Church in a way that the lay life cannot; but this does not mean that the lay life demands less dedication, less enthusiasm, less sanctity, less love. Nor does it mean that the refusal to live up to the lay vocation—the vocation of the baptismal vows—is basically any less wrong than the refusal of the religious vocation. Father Gerken insists that both the rich young man who refused what was in some sense the first religious vocation, and the layman who flees his calling are engaging in the lived No.

What a frightening notion, Nancy; one's whole life can be a gigantic No, a constant and consistent refusal to be what one ought to be, to be true to oneself and to God. And this kind of life can be lived—indeed, is being lived by many people—without committing any of the things that would appear in the normal category of sins. Yet there is hope:

This unhappiness, this unpleasantness, like all pain is a sign that real evil is present. Since unpleasantness is in the person, the evil

* *Ibid.*, p. 59.

is moral evil or sin. It remains in the person as long as the willful No remains. The only way this unpleasant experience can be removed completely is by a contradictory act, by a Yes. However, this Yes must not only be an acceptance of the invitation but also a rejection of, a reparation for the No. The answer must be at once love, contrition, penance. If it is not, then some of the unpleasantness will remain, some of the sin will remain.*

Kind of a frightening notion, isn't it, Nancy? And yet if there is anything I have learned from a decade of working with young people in our neighborhood, it is that Father Gerken is absolutely right: there is nothing worse than the lived No, nothing that more thoroughly destroys the human personality.

I am not suggesting that your life is a lived No. Surely on the basis of your generosity, your eagerness to respond to the promptings of grace in years gone by would preclude such an idea. But like everyone your age, your Yes is still highly tentative; there is still some hesitation, some element of the No in it. The No in your life—another way of describing infidelity—could very easily reassert itself. The doubts, the hesitations, the conflicts you have now are crucial. It would be so very easy for you to decide them with a No; indeed, you could do it almost without thinking, without even abandoning yet the trappings of a Yes.

Perhaps you don't really find this easy to believe. Yet I could list for you all kinds of people who have said No and are now, even in their very early twenties, living lives of negation. Their No doesn't even consist of a formal No to

* *Ibid.*, p. 116.

some kind of direct apostolic action. It could consist in refusing to leave home when it became clear that personal dignity and freedom could not survive unless one left home. It could involve breaking off a romance that had everything to commend it because of adamant parental opposition that was without any rational grounds. Or it could mean remaining in a romantic entanglement which was clearly unwise. It could mean refusing to finish college simply because one had grown tired of school. It could mean dating someone because of the fear of going a few weeks without a date. It might even consist in permitting a romantic rivalry to destroy friendship. The ways we can say No are limitless, although there are degrees of finality in the way we say No. However, enough little No's eventually add up to a big one. If we keep refusing to follow the inspirations of grace long enough, we harden our hearts to its promptings and the No becomes the measure of our personality.

And we always say No, Nancy, with the best possible excuses. We can think of so many reasons, so many justifications, so many explanations. I have never witnessed such ingenuity as that which the young people in our community display as they try to justify their infidelity, their No. They don't convince anyone, of course; not us when we hear them, not God, not even themselves—at least not at the deeper levels of their personality; but they surely provide an effective temporary silencer of conscience.

As I think I mentioned in another letter, a feminine No is in a way worse than a masculine No because it cheats the world out of more love. Yet the feminine No is easier to say,

because a girl can persuade herself that by giving herself to
her family she is really saying Yes, even though she has said
No previously to the possibility of full human development.
Girls can kid themselves into thinking that they can be feminine without first being human. There is a new book called
The Feminine Mystique by Betty Friedan that points out
the reason for this (even though I don't think we would go
along with everything that Mrs. Friedan says):

It is my thesis that the core of the problem for women today is
not sexual but a problem of identity, a stunting or evasion of
growth that is perpetuated by the feminine mystique. It is my
thesis that as the Victorian culture did not permit women to
accept or gratify their sexual needs, our culture does not permit
women to accept or gratify their basic need to grow and fulfill
their potentialities as human beings, a need which is not solely
defined by their sexual role . . . but by choosing femininity over
the painful growth to full identity, by never achieving the hard
core of self that comes not from fantasy but from mastering
reality . . . girls are doomed to suffer ultimately that bored diffuse
feeling of purposelessness, non-existence, non-involvement with
the world that can be called anomie or lack of identity, or merely
felt as the problem that has no name.*

Marriage itself cannot be a Yes unless it is part of a
larger human and Christian Yes. It is rather a No masquerad-
ing as a Yes, a selfishness pretending to be love, a lie dis-
guised as truth, an escape from reality claiming to be mature

* From *The Feminine Mystique*, by Betty Friedan. Copyright ©
1963 by Betty Friedan. Reprinted by permission of the publisher, W. W.
Norton & Company, Inc., New York, N.Y. Page 77.

realism. As one psychiatrist put it, "no one should get married who is unhappy as a single person, who is marrying from emotional hunger or sexual despair. We don't marry in order to become happy. We marry to become happier, which is different." And I might add a footnote to that statement. We don't date to become happy, but to become happier; we don't date because we cannot get along without dates, but because dates enhance a security and a confidence that is already part of us.

As I read back over this letter, I can't escape the impression that I sound as though I am trying to wake you up with a jolt by shouting at you. This would be rude as well as pointless. The alternatives to a Yes are indeed unpleasant, but if they are not obvious to you as you look around, no ranting from a clergyman is going to make them obvious. Fear is a good motive, I guess, up to a point; but it is only the beginning of wisdom. Instead of threatening you with the evils of a No, I suppose I ought to describe the advantages of a Yes. Yet even the beginnings of wisdom are not without some importance. Since I usually have a hard time being positive for very long, let me copy one more quotation from Father Gerken:

'Speak, Lord, your son is looking for your will and wants to do anything and everything you have planned for him.' This is the attitude of the Christian at Baptism. Any other attitude is fundamentally unnatural, because the individual is made not only for essential beatitude but for total personal love of God. Therefore, there must be in the core of the person an openness for anything and everything that God might ask of him. The person cannot

limit himself and say, 'speak, Lord, but speak only of essentials
and generalities, don't mix into details of my life, don't direct me
into areas where I have to give up money, recognition, a good
life. Let me conduct my life within the broad outlines of the
natural law, the ten commandments, the positive law of the
Church. That is hard enough, that is sacrifice enough, that is as
much as I choose to give you.' Such a limitation, such a cutting of
God out of the details of life, such an attempt to be alone and
independent, is unnatural and therefore wrong. Man must open
himself up to God because his concrete nature is open to the
infinite and transcendent God. Man must assent to this reality of
his own being. The commandment to love God with one's whole
heart is a verbal expression of the structure of man's concrete
being. Any limitation that is put on love must be removed because such a limitation closes man off from the Infinite. . . . Since
this is the goal of man, no one has the right to be a mediocre
Christian. . . . There are and can be no mediocre people in
heaven. They love God with the totality of their being—or else
they are not there.*

So that is the offer that the Lord is making to you,
Nancy. You either say "Yes" and love with all your powers
and in all your actions and thus be true to yourself, or you
say "No" and hesitate, procrastinate, and become mediocre
and unhappy because you have not been yourself. Someone
has defined man as a being who must love or perish; you cannot love if you are unfaithful to yourself. You did not turn
your back on this kind of love when you decided that a religious vocation was not yours. You merely decided that you
could find the peace which is a sign of progress in love in

* Gerken, *op. cit.*, pp. 147-148.

another way of life. You did not necessarily choose the inferior in preference to the superior, the mediocre in preference to the sublime, the less generous in preference to the more generous. You merely chose a somewhat different path, another way of being yourself, or orienting your personality towards God.

In the final analysis, Nancy, you must be Nancy and no one else. You cannot be what your parents want you to be, or what Peggy and your other sisters want you to be, or what your suitors want you to be or what your friends want you to be, or even what the nuns and priests who have crossed your path want you to be. At some point you must in effect tell the rest of us to go jump in the lake, and then make your own decision. You must say your Yes in your own way and in your own good time. I should rather like to be around when it happens, however; because the kind of happiness that the Lord will grant you is not especially common in the world.

Well, I have rambled on too long. Thanksgiving time draws near and attempts will be made to stir the Organization into activity, though if the truth be known Case's being in Washington and John's being in Paris have paralyzed us much less than I would want to tell those worthy gentlemen.

See you,

The Marriage Mania

Dear Nancy,

I gathered from your comments during our very brief encounter the day after Thanksgiving that you were somewhat puzzled by the comments in my last letter about marriage being in some circumstances a No, an infidelity to vision. Well, I guess I am somewhat pessimistic about romance, but it certainly seems to be one of the best destroyers of vision I know about.

For some young people, the Vision does not last very long, a few days, a few hours perhaps; for others it may survive for several years, but by the early twenties only a handful still seem to have it. However, there is one very interesting phenomenon which I only partly understand. In the late teens girls are more likely to have the Vision than boys, but girls lose it more quickly and boys are somewhat more likely to keep it. Thus, if you take a group of freshmen in college, you will find that far more of the girls are seriously interested in their lay vocation than the boys. But if you come back in four years, you will find that most of the girls

33

have proved unfaithful to the Vision, while a few boys still have it and indeed see it more clearly.

I can think of several reasons why girls in their late teens are more enthusiastic than their male contemporaries. Girls mature earlier, find the adolescent experience less confusing, begin to think for themselves at an earlier age, become skilled at abstract thought before boys. Furthermore, girls need worry less about earning a living and so can approach the "cultural" aspects of their education with more interest than can the boy who must worry about how his studies will affect his potential position in the job market. One will find a much more serious and intense intellectualism at a girls' college than at a boys' college.

But why the greater infidelity to the Vision among girls? One reason may be that the Vision is more superficial among the female of the species; she has arrived at it with less effort, so it is likely to be less profound. However, there are many social and cultural reasons for this lack of fidelity. The reason which contains within itself many of the others is what I would call the "marriage mania."

Now, Nancy, you know me well enough to understand that I am not opposed to marriage or motherhood. But for the record let me take a loyalty oath and affirm that I do not now hold theories opposed to matrimony and parenthood, nor have I ever held such theories. However, I am violently opposed to the manner in which these responsibilities are approached in our society and to the popular attitudes about what marriage can and cannot do in the life of a woman.

I suppose the best way to begin this subject is to remind

you of a talk one of your friends was compelled to give at a vocation week in high school. The subject was "The Role of Woman—Motherhood: Spiritual or Physical?" The theme of the talk was simple: you can be a physical mother if you get married, but you can be a spiritual mother if you become a nun; thus even in the religious life you will be able to fulfill your feminine role. Leaving aside the dubious notion that there is no spiritual element in physical motherhood (or that there is no physical element in spiritual motherhood), I would like to submit that the notion that motherhood is *the* feminine role is nonsense and is in fact dangerously close to heresy.

Before you dismiss this last statement, Nancy, as another one of my wild and outlandish theories, let me point out that I am not denying that motherhood and all that it implies are an extremely important and satisfying part of the life of a woman—though I suspect that to some extent both the importance and satisfaction are culturally conditioned and that in some societies the importance and satisfaction are less than in ours. Surely some of the talk identifying the role of woman with motherhood might be justified on the grounds that it does not intend to exclude other roles; perhaps not, but the other roles are never mentioned or are reduced to some kind of secondary importance. Now I should think that it is one of the basic truths of our faith that you are a human being, a Christian, a citizen, before you are a wife or a mother, and that the obligations of the former roles do not cease to exist when the latter are taken on. Marriage may specify the obligations flowing from baptism and confirmation, but it does not abrogate them. You are still consecrated to the apostolate of the Church by the prior sacraments and you are not excused from this consecration merely because you have entered a marriage contract. As one friend of ours puts it, "This is not the Soviet Union, and I am not going to get any medals just for bearing children."

What I am maintaining is that a woman can be happy without marriage and without children; it may be more difficult, of course, though for some people it may also be more easy. You can be fully a woman before you are married (indeed, you better be or you won't be much of a wife) and fully a woman if you should lose your husband. You can be happy before you have children, or after your children are dead, or even if you cannot have children. You can survive and you can survive very happily without husband and children and you can survive as a happy *woman*. You need not be afraid that you will feel useless or unfulfilled or unloved or unlovely. Indeed, let me make the statement even stronger: if you are not the kind of person who cannot survive emotionally as *a woman* without being a wife or a mother, then you are not the kind that will make a good wife and mother.

I am sure you realize, Nancy, that I am not urging the single state upon you. What I am saying is that you should not expect too much from marriage; in fact, paradoxically, the less you expect the more you will get from it. So many girls put all their emotional resources into the marriage relationship because they have come to believe that it is the only thing which will make them happy. They have no other important interests, no other satisfactions, nothing else to fall back on; marriage must satisfy all their wants and needs or they will not be happy. Now this is putting far too heavy a burden on the marriage relationship. Of course, marriage will be an important source of happiness to you, in some ways the most important; but it cannot be the only one. If you feel that you are going to find everything in marriage, you will succeed only in losing yourself. Indeed, it is the girl who is able to maintain a reserve about her expectations from marriage who will be happier in marriage. Because she has reached that state of maturity where she knows that she can survive as a person and as a woman without marriage, she is therefore able to bring more to marriage and will as a result get more from marriage. Because she has interests other than marriage, the marriage will be more interesting. Because she does not depend upon her husband and family completely, she has more to give to them. Because she is concerned about the whole world, she is able to be more concerned about her family. Because her love stretches beyond the walls of her home, it is stronger within the home. Because she is not a weak, cringing creature who is nothing when her husband or family are absent, she means much more to them when they are present.

My argument, Nancy, is that unless a girl is strong enough emotionally and mature enough as a woman to be able to face the prospect of not getting married, then she has no business in getting married because she is not capable of being a good wife or mother and indeed is not even capable of making a good choice of a husband. Marriage is not a merger of weaknesses; it is not a relationship where two lonely and dependent persons, who could not survive without each other, join forces hoping that their deficiencies will cancel out. Marriage is not a union of need with need, but of strength with strength. It is a pooling of resources rather than a pooling of dependencies. Only when you are quite prepared to be a spinster unless you find what you want in a husband are you ready to get married, because only then are you an adult woman. By these standards I suppose most people would never get married; it would slow down the propagation of the species but it would also notably curtail the amount of unhappiness and misery in the world.

A lot of people find this "marriage mania" terribly funny. While it certainly has some ludicrous aspects, I for one am not amused, because I think I have some notion of how it tears the souls of the people affected by it. What is happening is that the Vision is disintegrating. The girl has seen very clearly that she must love and be loved if she is to be happy; now she fears that if she does not move quickly to obtain the love of someone, then her chances for love will be forever blighted. There will be literally nothing else for her to do. She must forget all other kinds of love, so that she can concentrate on this one kind before it is too late. And it is often very difficult to relinquish the many enthusiasms of her younger years because they have been so satisfying, especially when she wonders, though perhaps very vaguely, whether what she is pursuing is really love. I suspect a lot of people succumb to the marriage mania only with a very guilty conscience; some of them will never get over the guilt (and increasingly there comes a time in later years when they try to escape it with neurosis or a bottle).

Yet one can understand their position. They want so intensely to have some one, or more accurately to belong to some one; and they do not have the courage to admit that they cannot belong to someone until they belong to themselves. They cannot find security in someone else's love until they are secure in their own self-confidence and self-realization. It is precisely this terrible longing for security that forces people into relationships in which they are absolutely certain in their more rational moments that they should not be involved. A girl will never find security, Nancy, by looking for it. This is the ultimate tragedy of the marriage mania: in a desperate search for love people look in precisely the wrong place.

The marriage mania reaches its heights during the middle and late years of college. Fear of spinsterhood seems to get its icy grip on the heart of practically every girl this age. The more honest ones will admit that panic has set in. Have you ever noticed how all the girls in a group tend to get their rings at about the same time? Optimists say how nice it is that there were such happy coincidences. Cynics say that the girls timed it that way and their husbands-to-be never knew what happened. Both are wrong. As members of the group begin to acquire their rings, as the bride books appear around the residence halls, as nuptial talk becomes the exclusive conversational subject, those who are not yet part of "trophy club" begin to get anxious; the gang is slipping away and soon they may be the last one. They may be the old maid of the group. Since this is a fate obviously worse than death, steps must be taken to see that a trophy is acquired or at least a promising boy. Otherwise there is simply nothing left to talk about.

As a result of the marriage mania, everything else becomes unimportant. Girls this age tend to be totally uninterested in anything else—school activities, studies, politics, the apostolate, all go down the drain. And the Vision, oh yes, the Vision—well maybe after marriage we can do something about it.

This is, of course, silliness. Statistically most girls marry. There is no need to get married young. Indeed, the odds are against your getting married only if you wait till 35. Some women are going to be happily married only if they wait till 25 or 30—or even 35 or 40. I am not against people getting married in their early twenties, but I am against them panicking into marriage at that age because of fear of loneliness, especially when they are not mature enough to know what kind of a choice they are making. And I am solidly opposed to the marriage mania causing them to be unfaithful to their Vision.

The marriage mania is hard to resist because it is so much part of the atmosphere in which girls your age live; this fear that they will be no one unless they become breeders of children may abate a little after graduation, when a few years of experience and observation persuade those that are left that some things are worse than spinsterhood. But by this time for many people it is too late.

A sure cure for the marriage mania, Nancy, would be to listen to a tape recording of "marriage cases" that come to rectories every week. Here were two people who were once young and thought they were very much in love. They had a beautiful wedding and their friends said what a lovely couple they were and everyone predicted much happiness for them. Even now perhaps to their neighbors and friends they look like an ideal couple; yet they are going through a living hell. It is not that either of them is bad or depraved; it is just that they married before they were mature and have never grown up. They made a wrong choice, a terribly wrong choice, the imprudence of which should have been clear to anyone at the time, and they are now not strong enough to live with this choice. They thought they were in love and they were only exploiting each others' dependencies much as sophomores in high school would. For such exploitation they must now pay the price.

If you look around at many of the so-called romantic relationships in which your friends are involved, you will notice that basically they are exploitive. Two people are using each other to satisfy their hungry longing for security. Two very dependent people are leaning on each other and one wonders how long it will be before they collapse. In the boy's case it is obvious; the relationship enables him to do to someone he takes to be a woman some of those things that men do to women (up to and perhaps beyond the limits of the moral law). Therefore he can assure his own weak male ego that after all he is a man. With the girl the case is not so obvious; she needs someone to assure her that she is important, someone to write her letters when she is lonely, someone who will take her out on dates when her friends have dates (lest she face the awful fate of doing nothing on a Friday evening), someone she can be sure of when the school dance rolls around, someone who will guarantee that the Christmas vacation will not be a failure. The major difficulty with this exploitive relationship is that people begin to confuse it with love.

One of the great emotional gifts a girl has, Nancy, is the gift of sympathy—the ability to "suffer with" other people. Your emotional resources are healthy and powerful; this is surely one of the reasons you are so popular with your contemporaries. It is difficult for people to come in contact with someone like you and not feel, "There is someone who understands me and likes me and wants to help me." But like all good things, strong emotions can be dangerous; every natural ability must be disciplined and restrained if it is not going to be as wild and turbulent as an unruly child. It is easy for a girl to be carried along by the surging tides of her emotions, and feel that since the emotions are so noble and generous they can do her no harm or lead her into no evil. She realizes that this is not true, that it is only disciplined and controlled emotions that are worthy of a human being, and that human love flows not merely from a frenzy of emotions but from the clarity of insight provided by that specific human faculty, the intellect. But the bubbling joy that comes from strong emotions often makes the intellect seem a rather pedestrian faculty. What she forgets is that when the intellect abdicates (or is forced into exile), she will be like a blind person driving a truck: if she does not end up in a crash which will injure herself and others, it will be because of special providential protection.

Even if she does not end up in a crash, she is running
the risk of letting the sweet emotions of youth turn into the
sour bitterness of middle age. While the emotions of a young
girl are appealing, they are not based on much more than the
physical freshness of the beginning of life. If she is unable
to root these emotions in the hard ground of firm intellectual
commitment (or should I say faith?), then she is going to
witness their premature death. The ability to inspire will
deteriorate into the necessity to nag; sympathy will turn to
harshness, kindness to cynicism, gentleness to coldness, compassion to nastiness, faith to shrewishness, and sensitivity to
prudery. These are the vices which we often lump under the
title "old maid," though you certainly have been around
enough to know that they can be just as common in the
married state. The next time you encounter a woman who is
sour and bitter and hard, you might say to yourself, "She
was once like me, and, in the absence of emotional control,
I will some day be like her."

It is said that love is blind; it most assuredly is not.
There is nothing that sees more clearly than love. But exploitation is blind; it does not see that it is using another
person, that it does not know the other person, that it really
does not care to know the other person. But exploitation is
habit-forming and as unhealthy dependencies grow stronger,
the boy and girl become certain that they are in love and so
in a haze of excitement and passion (should I have better
said lust?) they sweep down the aisle of the Church accompanied by the cheers of family and friends. They have married strangers. They may have been lucky or at least not too

unlucky; they may not be very happy, but at least they will be able to adjust to a low level of happiness or rather a low level of unhappiness.

What happens to the Vision in the process of converting dependency relationships into marriage? It gets lost in the shuffle, of course. I know of one Catholic Action organization in a coed college that lost its most dynamic member to an ex-seminarian who wanted no part of Catholic Action. He made the choice very clear to the young lady; it was either he or Catholic Action. She chose him and wrote a very touching letter of resignation to the priests in charge in which she thanked them for all their help in the past. Poor girl, she'll end up hating her husband for what he cheated her out of.

It is rare indeed that the apostolate can survive the acquiring of an engagement ring. It would seem, of course, that if people really had the Vision, they would make sure that their prospective partner did too; but few of them do. They are ready to settle for almost anything. Especially tragic is the case where two people have the beginnings of the Vision and they blot it out in each other, because the role-playing that courtship and engagement demand never permit them to let the other know where they really stand. It is ironic that two people on the verge of maturity actually destroy maturity in each other, because in their haste they are unable to practice the restraint and the control necessary to enable the other to develop into the kind of man or woman who would make a good wife or husband.

It seems to me, Nancy, that this is the most important moral question that people can ask about their romantic relationships: am I helping him to develop into a mature Christian? Is our relationship such that we are matching strength rather than need? Am I promoting the Vision in him and he in me? Or are we merely using each other as conveniences, conveniences that will become so useful that we will not want to dispense with them—unto death do us part? The morality of a relationship cannot be judged by a stop watch, a measuring tape, a biology textbook. Far more important than specific acts is the psychological climate of the relationship. Is it mutual exploitation of dependencies or is it promotion of restraint and maturity? In the old French proverb which I fear I have quoted to you far too often, is it "two people looking at each other or is it two people looking together in the same direction?"

At this point, Nancy, I hasten to assure you that I am accusing you neither of falling victim to the marriage mania nor of being unfaithful to your Vision and to yourself. Rather the contrary: I think that so far you probably have managed to remain faithful and to void the mania. But you should be under no illusions that it is going to be easy to resist the temptations that are going to increase all around you during the next couple of years.

Romance will certainly come to your life, Nancy, great love of the kind you have always dreamed; but do not push, do not hunt it down relentlessly, do not compulsively look for it with every boy you meet. It will come gradually and slowly, and it may take you years to find it or at least to discover it. Do not be frightened by loneliness or insecurity into abandoning your search, into settling for something much less than you know you must have. Look not for weakness you can mother nor for force which will overpower your identity. Look rather for strength which will match your strength, for maturity which will supplement your maturity, for vision which corresponds to your vision. Do not expect perfection for you will never find it (though neither will he, if the truth be told); but make certain, absolutely certain, that you agree about the purposes of life, the ideals to be pursued, the apostolate in which to work. Look long, look carefully, and I am sure you will find what you are looking for. Until then, be patient, be confident, and do not get too involved, because it is always painful to get uninvolved.

I am not saying that you will not be more attracted to certain boys than to others; this is part of the search and surely it would not be strange that one young man should at a given time be on your mind more than others—though I really think you are better off if you find two or three contending for top billing. And when the time comes that you begin to suspect that you have found the kind of person you have been looking for, remember that there is no rush. Long engagements can be very bad, but a long period of an "understanding"—perhaps unspoken—in which two people continue to be very independent and yet concerned about each other, can be very helpful for some people. This is the sort of relationship which most frequently happens in the post-college, graduate school period, when people are less in a rush and when involvement is approached in a much more leisurely—and to my way of thinking—more Christian fashion.

Well, enough about the marriage mania. I have already

spent too much time on it, falling victim to the very thing I condemn. Yet while I argue that marriage is not the only thing that is important in your life, I would not dream of denying that it is important. It is so important that it can either salvage your Vision or destroy it. It usually does the latter, but this is not the fault of marriage, rather only of the people who get married.

God bless,

The Dynamics of Sex

Dear Nancy,

It would seem that my remarks about the "marriage mania" stirred up some controversy among your friends; if the comments you quote are typical, I must have hit on a very painful subject. You know me well enough to know that I am not going to back down; but I am prepared to admit that the things I said in the last letter are rather negative, that I did not stress the "positive aspects" of sex and marriage. But I would argue that the reason for this is that what passes for love in our neighborhood so often interferes with the "Vision" that there are very few examples where it does not. I guess when you see things from the viewpoint of a parish priest you can get rather pessimistic; you see so many people messing up their lives that you tend to forget that there are some people who do not. My old buddy, G. K. Chesterton, said that in marriage some people succeed in finding each other while others only manage to lose themselves. I fear that the latter are more common, but it does not have to be that way.

But some positive things must be said if only to dispel

49

the notion that my cynicism is incurable. You remember the YCS moderators' committee we had last summer, which attempted to solve the problem of what could be done about the lack of sex education for the high school age level. (Incidentally the utter failure of that group is an interesting comment on the state of society.) I thought that we had come up with some pretty interesting ideas before the committee fell apart. Not the least important was the view of sex as a dynamic force in the human personality, an aspect of a man or a woman that brought vigor and strength and warmth to the character. This is a pretty good way to look at the subject since it does not tie sex down to certain organs or certain actions or even certain dizzy romantic emotions, but rather sees it as something which imparts tone and direction to the total personality. Sex then is not something to be ashamed of, much less something to be exploited, but rather a resource which breaks us out of the hard shell of selfishness and indifference.

It is easy enough to see how sex strengthens the personality of a boy; even though much of the romantic poetry about inspiration is, to put the matter charitably, exaggerated, there is a hard core of truth in it: you like to impress the one you love. As I observed in a letter to a certain young man, he was much more strongly motivated to go for the home run last softball season while the appropriate members of the opposite sex were looking on. On a somewhat more mature level, we certainly know that much of the sacrifice a husband makes on the job is for his wife (or at least he will claim it is). One of the most impressive stories I ever read about this power of sex in a time of crisis was by a flyer whose plane was shot down during the Second World War. The shock of the crash dulled his reactions; the warm water of the Pacific seemed so peaceful and comfortable; he was about to sink into a lethargy which would certainly mean death, when suddenly he thought of his wife and made a tremendous effort to break free of his seat belt and fight his way to the surface and to life. If it had not been for the fleeting thought of a girl half way around the world, he certainly would have died. She saved his life as surely as though she had been swimming beside him in the Pacific.

Since we usually don't think of strength as a feminine characteristic, it might be a little more difficult for us to realize how sex strengthens the personality of a girl. However, what I am trying to get at might become clearer if I say that mature sex adds depth to the character of a young woman. I know, Nancy, that you will not be offended if I say that girls in their early teens are often a superficial lot. They are sweet and charming and all that, but they have no more staying power than does the latest rock and roll idol whom they are currently worshipping. They are in love constantly but never consistently; they flit from one crush to another—usually with dream gods who correspond only slightly to the boys who supposedly resemble these gods. An innocent passenger who boards a bus carrying them to or from school cannot escape the impression that he is surrounded by thousands of jabbering, giggling monkeys.

Am I being too harsh on them? Not really, because the superficiality of the early adolescent girl is part of the devel-

opmental process. Her silly crushes, her falling in and out
of love with the speed of a revolving door are merely part
of her growing up. Her romantic daydreams are the result of
the fact that she is just beginning to learn how to love, to
experiment tentatively with her own emotions and the
responses of others to those emotions. She may do some
pretty stupid things, but they are usually innocent mistakes;
she is too superficial to be malicious—or to make sacrifices.

I would argue that sex—as opposed to ethereal fantasy
romances—deepens the personality of the girl by providing
her with the vigor to make sustained sacrifices for the one
she loves. The sophomore girl is still in love with a dream
that exists within her technicolor imagination; sex takes her
out of this dream and forces her to concentrate her attention
on another person who exists in the world of reality. Instead
of dissipating her emotional energies in transient crushes,
she now is able to focus them on one person. It is precisely
this focusing of emotional energies which enables her to
complete the final transition to maturity. Without the force
of sexual attraction it is reasonable to assume that a girl
would always remain a sophomore, always in love with the
most popular recording star. Unfortunately, some women
never discover mature sex and remain emotional sophomores
all their lives.

Paul Claudel has a very beautiful play, called *The Satin
Slipper*, which takes this notion as one of its major themes
(the other being the famous bit about God drawing straight
with crooked lines). Claudel's idea is that without sex we
would never learn to love other human beings, and without

loving other human beings we would never learn to love God. Sex is the "wound" in the personality which opens it up to the possibility of love. And I would add that it makes that love something strong and powerful instead of something weak and transitory.

Now from this point of view, I think, Nancy, that it becomes pretty clear the role sex has to play in the Vision. No matter how bright it may be, the Vision normally lacks depth in the ordinary young person. Sex adds a new dimension to the Vision, a third dimension which takes it out of the book and the classroom and puts it into the midst of reality— a reality often cold and harsh, but also potentially warm and friendly. "To seek God alone in the darkness might well be a terrifying thing; to embark on the journey hand in hand with one you love is to rob the journey of many at least of its terrors." Sex can (and usually in my observation does) cause people to say their final No; it can also serve to reinforce and make definitive a Yes. Our Vision demands that we give; sex teaches us how to give (or at least it was designed to do so). To say "Yes" demands that we be able to make sacrifice; sex forces us to make sacrifices but also provides us with the strength required for sacrifice. It can—and often does—drag a person into the depths; but it can also exalt him (or her) to the stars.

I cannot describe what sex ought to be doing in the life of a young person without thinking of what it so often does. Even if we pass over all the sins and the selfishness that pose under the name of love, we can't ignore the terrible narrowness that sexual attraction often introduces into the life of a young person. I remember one very talented young lady in the parish many years ago; she was intelligent, pretty, capable—and an incurable romantic. She was always deeply in love with someone; indeed she couldn't survive, it seemed, without being involved with someone—and often it seemed that it really didn't matter too much who that someone was. She periodically put in appearances at our Catholic Action meetings (which I admit were pretty primitive in those days). But you could never count on her, because you could never tell when her latest flame would whistle and she would have to come running; and, of course, her flames were never interested in very much of anything. She got into college and settled down on a semi-permanent basis with one particular boy. Suddenly she showed up one Sunday afternoon at a meeting of one of the groups which was an ancestor of The Organization, announcing to all that she had at last made up her mind that she was going to get involved in the lay apostolate and do something positive and constructive with her life. Her contribution to the meeting was—to say the least—dazzling. Afterwards I thanked her for coming around and complimented her on the brilliance of her insight. She assured me that I could count on her work from that point on and that she would be back for every meeting for the foreseeable future. I was young enough and naïve enough to believe her. Needless to say, she never showed up again. The truth of the matter was that the week before her appearance out of the mists, she and the boy friend had broken up; the following week they patched up their differences and that was the end of her career in the lay apostolate. Sex,

which ought to have broadened and deepened her personality, had in reality kept it narrow and shallow. She's a nice
girl, but I don't think she will ever know how to love. Sex,
instead of strengthening her love, made it impossible, because it kept her from becoming herself.

Now I am not even remotely suggesting, Nancy, that
you are going to do the same thing. I think such an event
most unlikely; but you must be honest enough to admit the
danger, to concede even that it would be so very easy to
confuse the pseudo-warmth of selfish infatuation with the
real warmth of generosity, to think that because you are
about to give your life to one person you are excused from
giving it to anyone else. If you do permit that confusion to
dominate you, you won't even be able to give yourself to
one another because, to be perfectly honest, you won't have
anything to give.

Some of the people in Catholic marriage education
circles have come up with marvelous sounding mysticism
about sex. (I suspect that they have cribbed it from the
French who can make anything sound mystical.) I don't
necessarily disagree with this mystical approach; human love
surely has something transcendental about it. But in my
perhaps biased observations, marriage can be a pretty difficult and demanding relationship; however, when sex and
love are so mixed as to be inseparable and even indistinguish-
able, the two people involved really don't mind the difficulties or the sacrifices. They have been forced out of their
selfishness and into the arms of another who is not an object
but now a person. The discovery of another person has

brought them such happiness that the hardships involved in continuing the discovery do not seem to matter. Having discovered each other, they are now in a position to discover the rest of mankind; indeed, they must or they will soon lose each other. "There are married couples who are completely wrapped up in each other and yet stay alone throughout their lives. They are sufficient to themselves. To make this love truly human an essential factor is lacking, which is self-forgetfulness." I suppose that sex is at its best when it does make us forget ourselves; the only trouble is that first we must have a self to forget.

I hope, Nancy, that you don't feel that the mature sexuality which I have been describing is something that is required of you now. After all you are still only nineteen; the high school sophomore is pretty much a creature of the past, but she is still not completely dead. Nor at your stage of the game ought she to be dead. You are not ready to get married, not ready even to make a definitive commitment to one person. To put the matter rather inelegantly, you are still very much engaged in shopping around. That you should be going from "love" to "love" right now is to be expected and is a good thing, though you ought to be doing it in a much wiser and more sophisticated way than when you were fifteen. You should have better control of your emotions, be more in possession of your affections, keep your attachments under stricter restraint. By now you know that every fluttering of the heart is not to be regarded as a sign from heaven, that every dreamy half-hour is not a promise of a life of bliss. Furthermore you ought to be increasingly aware that there are emotions in the other person which are not to be trifled with. The sophomore really doesn't care what she is doing to her boy friend, because she is hardly aware of his existence as a person. But you should have become mature enough to know that even if you could never really love a certain boy, you must not let your emotional effervescence lead him on. The girl who is breaking the hearts of a long string of suitors is really a monster—or someone who is too dumb to know what she is doing. Of the two, I think the monster is probably better because she can always change.

It is within this context of sex as strength and depth that we must view the question of chastity. There is no doubt, Nancy, that the traditional Christian standards of sexual morality are something less than fashionable today. Premarital—and post-marital—chastity may never have been particularly popular in practice; but today there are rather few people who are willing to defend such customs even in theory. Sex is natural, whatever is natural is good, therefore there is nothing wrong with sex—or so the argument in its most simple fashion goes. One does not even have to believe in original sin, however, to see that things are not nearly that simple. Sex is not only natural, it is also extremely powerful— one might almost say demonic in its power. Every powerful natural force must be channeled if its unruly strength is not going to cause disaster. From the traditional Judaeo-Christian viewpoint, self-discipline—which is to say chastity—is nothing more than the harnessing and focusing of sex so that it will operate in the proper fashion, and not destroy the personality. Chastity is not negative and frustrating; rather it is extremely positive and enriching because it is disciplined use of a powerful ability—something remotely like the polished skill of a poet or a ballet dancer or a great painter who has learned how to focus his abilities under the restraint of a fully developed art. Chastity is not weakness; it is power.

Now in our particular community, Nancy, chastity still has some vogue, partly for social reasons and partly for religious reasons; yet there are still problems and I think that from the girl's side the major problem is a kind of phoney maternal tenderness that she can persuade herself is compassion. To be inelegant once again, sympathy opens a door in the human heart that you can drive a truck through. If a boy can persuade a girl that he needs her and depends on her, her independence is very likely to collapse. Restraint and self-control are often no match for undisciplined and unperceptive generosity. The girl who gives her heart to every passing "sufferer" is likely to end up by giving much more—especially when she herself is lonely and just a little curious.

Well, there I go again—being negative. Unfortunately I believe in sin and judgment and other such negative things; and I have the old-fashioned notion that the abuse of that which is splendid is one of the worst kind of abuses. And if I am forced to say which is worse—an occasional violation of the moral law or the destruction of a total personality through the inability to harmonize sex with love and vision— I will readily choose the latter as being much worse. But both are evil and of this we have too much.

God bless,

Love and Marriage

Dear Nancy,

Christmas was surely dismal. John was lucky to be in the hospital in Rome; I'm sure it was more fun than the Hills during this holiday season. However, the lay mission investigations seemed to be somewhat promising. I fear, however, that it is going to take someone working full time to get it organized.

I was intrigued by the question that came up at the party at Mary Kay's house—does anyone ever ask the parish priest whether they ought to get married? I don't suppose that they really ought to ask in just those terms; whether and whom one marries is a decision one must make for himself or herself. I can see the wisdom of consulting one's spiritual adviser before marriage, but most people don't have spiritual advisers and the role of the parish priest seems practically to be rather different. A few people have come around to the Rectory during the mating season, not so much to consult as to get confirmation of what they have already planned to do. Some others are really unsure and close to panic and they want the priest to make the doubts go away. It is rather

59

peculiar that those who ought to be having doubts rarely do and those who ought not to doubt are frequently troubled. Perhaps it is not surprising however; those who are mature enough to enter a wise marriage are also mature enough to see the possibility of a mistake; while those who are on the high road to disaster are blind even to the possibility of danger—many of them because they want to be blind.

I have never advised anyone not to enter a planned marriage and find it very difficult to imagine a situation where I would, though there are some cases where I might be tempted to point out the problems involved in a proposed match. But even such a relatively moderate procedure has so many dangers that I would be quite hesitant to use it often. In the final analysis people must make their own decisions, live their own lives, and suffer for their own mistakes; there's precious little that those of us in the older generation can or should do that will make them change their minds. In any event, you can count on this: you will never get any such advice from me. You are too intelligent to need and too strong-willed to follow it, if you were not going to anyway.

However, I will not hesitate to lay down some general principles about the selection of a spouse. They are so obvious that one wonders why they need be mentioned, except that they are so ignored so often in practice.

First of all, Nancy, you know very well that you both must have common values; husband and wife must want the same things out of life and be in general agreement as to how these things are to be obtained. In your case this is to say that the man you marry must have the Vision too. He need not use the same vocabulary to describe it, but he surely will have to be dissatisfied with the ordinary and the mediocre. His "Yes" might be to a slightly different set of propositions, but it must be a "Yes" to match yours both in intensity and direction. If he objects to your present apostolic activities or if he is unimpressed or unexcited about them, then you really don't want the same things out of life and will simply make each other unhappy. And you should be wary of the boy who discovers the apostolate when he discovers you. His interest may be sincere, but don't take that for granted. Make sure that he is not like the girl who becomes a hockey fan during courtship when she was not one before and has not the slightest intention of continuing to be one afterwards. Feigned interest in hockey may be rather harmless, but feigned interest in the Church is deadly because it has to do with crucial life values. If all your boy friend really wants is domestic peace in a comfortable suburb, comb him out of your hair because you will never bring him peace—nor much of anything else.

It should hardly be necessary to say that you should respect the boy you marry. One would think, Nancy, that a girl would not dream of getting involved with a boy whose character she did not admire; and yet a lot of other things can be confused with admiration—amusement, pity, fascination, sympathy. Are there aspects of his personality that you would not want your children to know about or that you would want to hide from your friends or your future neighbors? Is he irresponsible or superficial or unreliable? If he seems so to you now, then he certainly is and he is a poor risk—no matter how charming or personable he might also be. A boy may be hilariously funny, the life of the party, a superb clown, and still not be admirable. If you don't find him admirable in all the qualities you think important, then get rid of him as quickly as you can.

He should be at least as intelligent as you are. I don't mean that his marks need be in the same percentile as yours, but he must be able to keep up with you intellectually (and you with him). If you don't have serious interests in common, if you are incapable of having intelligent conversations now about things you both consider important, what in the world are you going to talk about after you are married? The truth is that you won't communicate on any level other than the physical—and as time goes on not even at that level. It is bad enough for a man when his wife is not capable of understanding what he is talking about or what he is doing in his work; it is far worse for him to know that he cannot understand what she is talking about or keep up with her brilliance. Nothing can so utterly demoralize a man as to know that his wife thinks he is stupid, especially when he realizes that by her standards he is. I am not advocating that you turn into an intellectual snob, but simply that you realize that it is not wise to marry anyone who is too different from you, especially when that difference has to do with a quality that is valued in our society as much as intelligence is.

You should further steer clear of someone whose life you can run. A lot of boys are looking for the girl who would be a good housewife—and by that they mean one who would be a good cook and housekeeper and children supervisor. The female equivalent of this syndrome is the search for a boy who will do what the girl wants him to do—any time and all the time. Such a girl wants to play the role of a queen bee and she would like to find a worker bee to run her errands and perform her chores. It is just not good for a girl to have a husband whose only posture towards her is one of adoration. The lad who is constantly on his knees before a goddess whom he is worshipping is likely to end up a doormat; and while doormats may be nice things to have around, they are no substitute for a husband. If a boy makes no counter-demands, if all he wants is what you want, then he is a doormat in the making.

Nor should you choose someone because you think you can make something out of him by reforming his life. If he has not made something out of himself, no girl is ever going to do it. If he is not someone, you are not going to turn him into someone. If both your personalities have solid inner cores, then, of course, they will develop and flourish under the influence of the warmth of love. But if there is nothing there to begin with, love isn't going to produce something, mainly because love is not possible. The notion that some girls have, that they can mold a boy into something he isn't, is the wildest kind of self-delusion.

To be very specific you should avoid like the plague the boy who drinks too much. If he isn't going to stop being a drunk during courtship, he certainly isn't going to stop after marriage. There is no easier way to cultivate a hell on earth than by marrying a potential alcoholic. Yet all kinds of women do just that, thinking that they are going to reform

the poor souse with their maternal love. They will do exactly
the opposite; their "kindness" will make the drunkard feel
even more guilty and drive him to more drink. In the process
it is not at all infrequent for the wife—and the children—to
turn into alcoholics too. There are all kinds of blindness
associated with what is defined as "love," but none more
incredible than blindness to potential alcoholism. Yet this
kind of blindness seems to be widespread. If a girl doesn't
want to face the fact that her fiancé is a souse, then she just
pretends he isn't. It is surprising how quickly problems can
vanish when you pretend they are not there; and when they
reappear it is usually too late to do anything about them.

Nancy, whatever you do, don't marry someone who is
looking for a mother. The world is filled with boys who have
never been able to stand on their own two feet and never
will. Their mothers have smothered them with attention and
service, and now they are looking for a girl who will replace
their mother and "take care" of them for the rest of their
lives. This sort of boy has all the force of character of a used
dishrag, but he is such a pitiable specimen that he appeals
to the "maternal instincts" of girls—much in the same way as
would a three-year-old with a running nose. Unfortunately
a lot of girls confuse the "maternal instinct" (which has
nothing to do with motherhood, by the way) with love, and
are doomed to spend the rest of their lives with an overgrown infant. If a boy cannot stand on his own feet, don't
let him lean on you because eventually the two of you will
collapse. Children are nice—especially when there is a man
around the house; but when the man is the worst of the

children, the home never gets beyond the chaos of an or-
phanage. It's always easy to spot one of these overgrown
infants, if you want to look at evidence. How does he relate
to his mother? Does she make all his decisions for him? Does
she pull the strings that make him jump? Does he find it
hard to get along without her total approval? If he does,
don't kid yourself into thinking that what you see is love; it
is dependency and is disgusting no matter how reverent it
may at first appear. This child with the body of a man might
be very charming and considerate; his mother has brought
him up well; his behavior is just beautiful. Indeed, he is the
perfect model of the "ladies' man"—which, of course, is
exactly what he is; only ladies' men do not make good husbands because they are not men, no matter how masculine
their carefully chosen apparel may make them look.

Be careful about falling for someone who is too different from you. Despite the slick magazine mythology about
love conquering all, it seldom does. The more similarity in
background and values between husband and wife, the more
likely the marriage is to be successful. Girls (and boys) go
through a stage when they are fascinated by the exotic and
the unusual in members of the opposite sex, and when they
think it is somehow liberal and noble and imaginative to
date someone who is from another world than their own.
Interesting it may be, but on a permanent basis it is hardly
likely to work.

I remember one charming, young lady who announced
to me—and not jokingly—that she would like to be swept off
her feet by an Italian count. I don't think she ever met any

Italian counts except in cheap movies and second-rate fiction, and I suppose she will leave that stage behind and marry someone from her own neighborhood. Yet I have a hunch that if a suitable-looking Italian count had arrived on the scene, she would have set out in pursuit of him. I am not saying, Nancy, that you should necessarily marry someone from the Hills, but if your husband-to-be would not fit in well with your friends, your family, and the community in which you grew up, there is an open question of will he fit in with you. We are pretty much what our environment has made us and if something is out of place in our environment, it is probably out of place in our lives. The old Chinese proverb, "You should take a wife from the house whose door is opposite your own," is sound advice for the choice of a husband too. It may sound dull to marry someone who might have been your cousin or even your brother because his life is so similar to yours; it is not really dull, but very wise.

Have naught to do with the young man who is drifting, who doesn't know who he is or where he is going or what he wants to do. I have in mind the kind who have been in two or three colleges, can't hold a steady job and can't fashion even a vague plan for their future. Everyone says, "Oh, he will settle down when he finds some nice girl." Perhaps, but there's no point in you being the "nice girl" that his friends and family select to "settle him down," because the odds are very much against him settling down, and you (or any other girl) are not going to be any help to him for very long.

Perhaps what I am saying through many of these rather negative paragraphs, Nancy, is that you must be careful that you are not deceived by your own very powerful affective emotions. There are all kinds of strong emotional reactions a girl can experience concerning a young man; many of them may look like love and sound like love, but they are only poor counterfeits. Don't be taken in by them, don't be blinded by them, don't let them impair your reason or your ability to take a hard, critical look at the young man in question to determine whether you really love, or whether you are simply in love with your own emotions.

As usual I have proceeded on the *via negativa,* talking about what you ought to avoid rather than what you ought to look for. But I suppose one could go through the last few pages and restate in a positive fashion what I have said. The boy you are looking for should have the same values you have, should inspire your respect and admiration, ought to be intelligent enough and strong enough to be the head of the family, mature enough to need a wife and not a mother and to face the problems of life without the crutch of alcohol. He should have a clear idea of who he is and where he is going, and it would be well if he came from a social and cultural background generally similar to the one whence you come. When stated this blandly, such qualifications seem to be so simple-mindedly obvious as to hardly need mention. Yet all you have to do, Nancy, is to look around the community and see how unobvious they are. The other day a girl was in to see me whose three best friends are getting married the same month she is; she was convinced that the others were all making mistakes and was wondering whether she was as blind as they were. She wasn't, but they certainly were, probably because they did not want to see. Don't think that this could not happen to you.

Yet it should not be so hard to find someone who measures up to the qualifications about which I have been writing. Even when you add the all important qualification that he ought to have the same vision of the lay vocation as you have, I am sure that there are many boys your age who would make excellent husbands. There is no such thing as the one true love, the "soul mate" for whom you must search until the day you hear bells ringing in your brain. You must look carefully indeed, but if you act with even a moderate amount of the intelligence with which God has blessed you, you will find what you are looking for (or discover it in something that you have already found) without any serious danger of messing up your life. The major problem will be keeping your emotions under the control of intelligence.

Are there any reality checks which will enable you to be sure that your emotions are not playing tricks on you? I can think of several. First of all, what are his friends like? A boy is probably not much different from those with whom he associates. If you find that you like him, but can't stand his friends, you ought to ask yourself if he is really that different from his friends or whether you may be fooling yourself. And if he has no friends, get him out of your mind as fast as you can. Don't let yourself be tricked by pity for someone who has no friends; if he lacks friends, it is his own fault and there is nothing you can do for him.

Secondly, what do your friends think of him? Now we

both know that girls (and fellows) are apt to be jealous at first when they see someone who is threatening to break up their crowd of friends. The new boy friend or the new girl friend is viewed as a rival and resented. Sometimes this resentment gets very cruel and bitter, but usually it passes and the "outsider" is accepted and even liked by the "crowd." The question is not what your friends think of him when he arrives on the scene, but rather what they think of him when they are over their jealousy and really get to know him. If they still don't like him, then you really ought to start to review the bidding. They may be wrong, but the odds are very much against it.

Another way of telling whether a marriage will be a happy one is so obvious that there is no reason to mention it, except that many people don't seem to be aware of its existence. On this matter perhaps above all others, you ought to listen to your family. Now I don't deny that some families get terribly possessive and do not want their children to marry, or at least do not want them to marry anyone who is not a handpicked choice of the family. However, I do not think that you have to worry about this; even though a good family like yours may show an initial scepticism about a potential suitor, I think that this is understandable. Parents want the very best for their offspring and ought to take a hard critical look at a potential son-in-law (or daughter-in-law). The important question you should ask is whether they like a suitor *after* they get to know him. If they do, then you can be assured that the marriage at least will never be a disaster. If they don't, well, they might be wrong, but the odds are very heavily against it. Parents usually know rather well who their daughter is and what is going to make her happy; if they take a dim view of a marriage, the match must at best be rated as very risky.

On this subject I have said enough. You will excuse me, Nancy, for being so calculating on an aspect of life which transcends all calculation. Perhaps I ought to end this letter with a very simple but quite accurate quotation from Edith Stein which leaves behind both romanticism and cynicism, "To share in another's life, to take part in all that concerns him, in the greatest as well as the smallest things, in joy and sorrow, but also in his work and problems, that is the wife's special gifts and her happiness."*

God bless,

---

* Cf. Edith Stein, *The Writings of Edith Stein* (Westminster: Newman, 1956) and *The Science of the Cross* (Chicago: Regnery, 1960).

Home or Career

Dear Nancy,

It is mid-semester here (and too bad about the rain in the mountains; it must make skiing difficult) and time for our high school seniors to start planning for next year, to sweat out applications, to worry about College Boards, to compete for scholarships, and, if they are girls, to plan their wardrobe.

Yet there is one different element this year, one that really surprises me. You will remember how there is always a "move" that is popular with each different senior class. One year St. Mary's is the place to go, another year Barat, another year Edgewood, another year your alma mater. This year the "move" is quite a bit different; it is not to go to college at all. The group that has come up with this scheme is by no means in the lower half academically either. But they argue that the main purpose of college is to help a girl be interesting to her husband and that they can be that if they read enough books. Hence there is no need to go to college and it would be much more fun to go to business school and

71

get a job in the business world as quickly as possible. There is no point in wasting time going to school.

The marriage mania at work again, you say? Not exactly, because these girls are not planning marriage quite yet. I think the problem rather is something that is more fundamental than even the marriage mania, and I would be tempted to call it the "housewife heresy"—the peculiar notion that by doing what a housewife does a woman is going to find fulfillment, that the chores of cooking, cleaning, dusting, and raising little children are the only things that really make a woman happy and that nothing else in life—except being "interesting" to her husband—is important for a woman.

Now I am sure that I don't have to persuade you, Nancy, of the prevalence of this heresy. You have heard it—usually in a somewhat less blunt fashion than I have phrased it—often enough to know that it is accepted as an article of faith by large numbers of girls your age. However, older people are hard to convince. Even my sister who is only six years out of college thinks I'm dreaming when I talk about housewifery. She admits that girls of her generation wanted to get married indeed, but few of them were particularly eager to be housewives. When I tell her that many supposedly intelligent young women of the present graduating classes are not really interested in anything else, she just can't believe it.

What has happened is that the pendulum has swung full cycle; the age of the career woman has been succeeded by the age of the housewife, and both of them have pretty much forgotten that a woman is also a human being. You were not around in the 1930's, Nancy, and you will find it difficult to believe that the "ideal" woman of that epoch was the "career" woman. The battle of the feminists for equal political and legal rights for women had been won in great part, and the female half of the republic was now free to enjoy its new privileges. Women were the equals of men and were able, it was argued, to compete with men in the world of business and profession. It was expected of the sophisticated girl that she join in the competition. Even if she married and had a family, her career was expected to go on. The monotonous tasks of housecleaning and cooking were to be subdelegated to less glamorous people than the "career woman," who was obliged to continue her contribution to the economy and society. Of course, not everyone did this; most people did not, but many of them wished they could. If you don't believe this possible, some day you ought to look at copies of the women's magazines of the 1930's and compare their heroines with the heroines of the 1960's. The contrast is enlightening; the change from career girl to suburban matron has been dramatic and complete.

It soon became clear to educators and therapists that the career girl, for all her glamor, was not at all happy. Her husband and family were just not enough to satisfy her when they were in a secondary position in her life. There was not enough love in the world of career to satisfy the average woman, and a marriage that was merely a part-time relationship didn't make up for the inadequacies of career. The wisdom of the old adage, "a woman's place is in the home," was rediscovered. It began to dawn on a lot of people that most women were not going to be happy unless they could devote a good deal of their life to raising children.

Now I have no quarrel with this insight; its validity for our society at least seems unquestionable. Unfortunately, it suffered the fate of many other valid insights; it got into the hands of people who did not understand what it really meant and oversimplified it so that it became absurd. The pendulum began to swing immediately after the Second World War in the surge of domesticity that marked the return of the GI's and the emergence of Suburbia, and reached its acme when *McCall's* began to preach the gospel of "togetherness." The result is that some utterly incredible things are happening. Advertising men have learned that women really don't want their household devices to be laborsaving. A completely push-button setup would cheat them out of the feeling of accomplishment which follows hard work in the kitchen. In one experiment 250 housewives were asked to choose among four imaginary methods of cleaning. The first was a completely automatic dirt removal system which needed no supervision. The second the housewife had to press a button to start. The third was portable; she had to carry it around and point at an area to remove the dirt. The fourth was a brand-new, modern object with which she could sweep away the dirt herself. (It was called a "broom" though the girls weren't told that.) You can guess which one was the most popular: the last. As one wife observed, "as for some magical push-button cleaning system, well, what would happen to my exercise, my feeling of accomplishment, and what would I do with my mornings?"

Yes, precisely, what *would* she do with her mornings?

Some of the time and motion studies have come up with similar findings. Housewives were in general terribly inefficient at their work, taking many more hours to do it than was really necessary; so much so that the dictum was coined, "housework expands to fill the time available." A woman is really afraid to get her work done, because when it is done there will not be anything else to do. She has been convinced that her housework is her fulfillment, and when it is done what happens to fulfillment? The housewifery mystique is nothing more than an easy way to escape from oneself, an oversimplified answer to the question of what meaning can be found in life, a pseudo-self-sacrificing excuse for maturity. The girl who argues that she is going to get her major life rewards out of housewifery is running away from the painful process of becoming someone in her own right; she is kidding herself into thinking that if she can submerge her personality in her work and her children, she can escape from the realization that she really does not have a personality.

Let's be perfectly honest about it: there is nothing rewarding about drudgery or monotony. The more the work of the woman of the house can be automated, the more opportunity she will have to become fully human, the more time she can devote to the human tasks of a wife and mother instead of having her time consumed in physical labor, which in other societies was done by slaves. The only trouble is that it is harder to be a free woman than to be a slave, because the free woman must put in intellectual effort and the slave need not. The girl who has been taken in by the housewifery heresy is not going to be satisfied with what she is doing, but she will really be afraid to try anything else because that would require maturity and this is one thing she doesn't have; better to compulsively wipe doorknobs.

While I am saying outlandish things, let me add that I think that some of the people engaged in Catholic marriage education (and I don't mean Chicago Cana) have bought the housewifery heresy completely. One can hear an awful lot of nonsense about the glories of homemaking if one listens to the right people. In fact, you even begin to suspect that they believe it, except you don't notice them engaging in much housework themselves.

Now before you call the local branch of the FBI to turn me in as Unamerican, let me be very clear about what I mean. First of all, I am not saying that the work of being a wife and mother is not challenging—especially those elements of the work which have to do with the education of children. Secondly, I am arguing that the work of the house-wife—especially the repetitive non-intellectual parts of it—is not enough to satisfy a woman's search for meaning and significance in life. Thirdly, I would even claim that if a woman does not have some kind of interests above and beyond the narrow demands of housewifery, then she isn't even going to be an efficient wife or mother—indeed, she will not even be much of a cook or a housecleaner and certainly not much of a human being.

To my first point, let me repeat the following famous quote from G. K. Chesterton:

To be Queen Elizabeth within a definite area, deciding sales, banquets, labors and holidays; to be Whitely within a certain area, providing toys, boots, sheets, cakes and books; to be Aristotle within a certain area, teaching morals, manners, theology and hygiene; I can understand how this might exhaust the mind, but I cannot imagine how it could narrow it. How can it be broad to be the same thing to everyone and narrow to be everything to someone? No, a woman's function is laborious, but because it is gigantic, not because it is minute. I will pity Mrs. Jones for the hugeness of her task; I will never pity her for its smallness.*

You will remember my earlier comment that I had no argument with the insight that most women are seeking the happiness of home and family; my argument rather is with those who think that this happiness can be equated with the more simple-minded tasks of peeling potatoes or washing dishes. Unquestionably such work can be a labor of love, but of themselves mechanical tasks have no dignity; there are much more human ways of expressing love, such as teaching children the meaning of music and art. The more monotonous work we can remove from the life of a woman, the more time she will have to play a truly human role in her relationships with her husband and children. The only problem with this is that she must be human to begin with, she must have something more to offer her family than cooking, dishwashing, sock-darning and nose wiping.

You see what is involved in this line of arguing, Nancy; if the most important things a woman does at home are human things, activities beyond the routine and the mechanical, it follows inevitably that she must have interests beyond the family, or she will have nothing specifically human to

* *What's Wrong with the World* (New York: Sheed and Ward, 1942), p. 153. This book was originally published by Dodd, Mead in 1910.

offer her offspring and husband beyond that which a slave or an automation system might offer. You can't teach art appreciation, unless you are interested in art; you can't train your children in charity unless you are concerned about racial hatred; you can't sustain your husband's concern about politics unless you think that is a valid area of human activity. You cannot listen sympathetically to an account of the impact of economic change on your husband's business, if the only economics you know is the cost of round steak ground. You cannot help your family to be a vital cell in the Mystical Body, if your only vision of the Mystical Body is teaching prayers to your children.

We hear much today about the problem of modern women. I think the problem can be summed up very succinctly: we have taken out of women's life most of the mechanical tasks which used to keep her in drudgery all day but at least gave her something to do that had to be done; but we have not replaced the mechanical tasks with satisfying human activity which will be centered in her husband and children, yet will not be confined to the family alone. Both the "housewife" and the "career woman" are attempts to escape from this problem, and they are attempts which are doomed to failure because they do not face the unescapable fact that you cannot be much of a career woman or a housewife unless you are a human being first.

In the absence of activity which stimulates her intellect, stirs her imagination, deepens her love for the good, the true and the beautiful, opens to her horizons beyond the confines of the kitchen and the back yard (or front yard in some suburbs), the woman of today is not going to be much of a wife and mother. She probably won't even be a good cook because it is rare that an unhappy woman will consistently provide good food; or if she does, her neurotic temperament will so upset her family's digestive systems that no one will enjoy the food.

The frustrated mother who thought she was going to find in "homemaking" a short cut to maturity is not going to be much of a help to her children. She will try to live her own life over in her children, enjoying vicariously what she has missed in her own life. But, not knowing specifically what she has missed, she will almost certainly steer her children down the wrong path too. She has never got beyond the infantile state herself and she will not let her children grow up either. She wants to keep her children for herself, since they are all she has (relations with her husband having deteriorated long ago). Therefore she keeps her children emotionally dependent on her, which is to say that they never mature beyond the infantile state. The maternal slave has turned into the devouring mother. By becoming the "all-loving and all-giving mother . . . she forces her children always to be the recipients; they become not only all-receiving, but also all-taking."* As a result, the children

are the victims of their mother's disordered maternal instinct; feeling that she has been cast in a role of heroic proportions, she throws herself into it, and apparently her children let her play it

* M. Esther Harding, M.D., *The Way of All Women* (New York: Longmans, Green, 1937), p. 195.

to the hilt. These are the children who, to the bystander, appear to be selfish little beasts, unconcerned about the devotion and goodness of their self-sacrificing mother. But she, not they, is the cause of their selfishness. She has misunderstood the demands of love and has forgotten that we are commanded to love others as we love ourselves. Her attitude toward herself lacks respect (she is the door-mat for her children) and it is no wonder that her love seems to fail to stimulate self-respect in her children and the ability to love their mother with respectful love in return.*

As one commentator put it, "This exclusive maternal love hides not infrequently unfulfilled desires, interior insecurity and aimlessness, a festering fear of life."†

I am sure, Nancy, that you do not want children like those I have just described. Then don't let the housewife heresy fool you. If you are not someone when you become a homemaker, and are not determined to remain someone even through the chaotic years when your children are young and make tremendous demands on your time and energy, then you are not going to amount to much as a person and neither will your children. They will be nothing but imitations of their mother, and since their mother is a hollow, empty person, they will be hollow and empty too. You may smother them with phoney affection, but they will hate you for the rest of their lives, since you were never able to give them an example in maturity because you never learned it yourself.

You are clever enough, Nancy, to spot the basic weak-

* Dorothy Dohen, *Women in Wonderland* (New York: Sheed and Ward, 1960), pp. 128-129.

† Eva Firkel, *Woman in the Modern World* (Chicago: Fides, 1956), p. 108.

ness of this letter. When I said that the problem of modern woman was to find significant and challenging human tasks centered in but transcending the family to replace the mechanical drudgery which modern technology has made necessary, I was not too specific about what these tasks might be. The reason I was not too specific is simple enough: I don't know what they are and I don't think anyone else is really sure. It will be up to your generation to find out for yourselves and blaze the trail for those who come after you. I have no doubt that you and many others like you will be equal to the task, especially if you don't let the cliché mongers and the slogan manufacturers fool you with second-rate substitutes for wisdom.

To end on a happier note, Grace Ann has volunteered to work full time next year on the lay mission project. This puts the operation back into high gear.

God bless,

Women and the Life of Learning

Dear Nancy,

So someone wonders whether Father Greeley thinks that the place of woman is in the home? The question is fair enough, I suppose, since I did use the phrase in my last letter, though I intended it to mean that a woman finds happiness in the home and can find it only with difficulty elsewhere (though it is perfectly clear that she can find it elsewhere). However, if the meaning of the phrase is not clearly specified, it becomes pretty empty. Does it mean that a woman has major concerns in and major satisfaction from home and family? If it does it is certainly true, but it would also be equally true of a man. Does it mean that a woman ought to have no major interests beyond the walls of her home? If it does it is arrant nonsense, at least for the young women of today. No human being, whatever the sex, has any right to secede from the human race. Does it mean that a woman will tend to spend more time in the home than a man—especially during the earlier years of the marriage? I would suppose that this statement is hardly questionable in most instances. Does it mean that the intelligence of a woman is to be trained mainly for the tasks of the home? If it does it will lead to disaster since the one who has been trained for work in the home only, won't even be good at that.

Intelligence in a woman—what a fascinating subject. Society urges girls to get good marks in school (and they do, better than boys in fact), but then warns against being too intelligent. Without even realizing it a girl tends to cover up her intelligence so that she will not threaten any of the males in her life (father, brother, suitor, husband, teacher). As a result various studies (including some we are doing at NORC*) tell us that girls in college are much less able to integrate a life of scholarship and a life of social activity than boys, because the two seem more contradictory to girls than to boys. High school boys are much more likely to want to be remembered as good students in their schools than are girls who put a higher valuation on popularity. The smart girl keeps her intelligence a secret, she is told; and often she is not even aware that she is doing it.

Which brings me to an incident from your own life that illustrates what I am getting at. Two years ago, when Case persuaded us that you and Fran were to be brought into the the YCS moderators' group, he argued that the two of you were among the brightest high school seniors he had ever seen. This was immediately evident, even at the first moderators' meeting when you took on Tod and reduced him to silence. I was duly impressed and commented several times during that summer and the following autumn to various of

* National Opinion Research Center.

your contemporaries on your intellectual abilities. The reaction I got was almost always one of puzzlement: Nancy
was a fine girl, yes; great personality and lots of fun, of
course, but brilliant intellectually, well, hardly. It finally
dawned on me that, when you were around the moderators
who were for the most part older than you and out of the
dating range (at that time), you were at ease intellectually,
but when you were with your own contemporaries, the image
you were projecting was quite a bit different. Now I am sure
that this was neither conscious nor deliberate, but simply the
normal way an intelligent girl feels she ought to act in her
late teens and early twenties.

I remember one young man in particular who thought
he knew you very well and was quite convinced that the
poor old parish priest didn't know what he was talking about.
Then I guess one night he goaded you just a little bit too
far and you turned on the brains. The result for him was
traumatic. Indeed, he had not recovered the next day when
he reported to me, "Hey, you were right; she really is
brilliant." The point of this story is that the sudden display
of your intellectual ability didn't hurt his opinion of you at
all. He was dazzled, but he was impressed. For the first time
he began to understand who you really were.

I am trying to make a case that girls should not try to
hide their intelligence, even though I realize that all the
cultural patterns go against what I say. It is true that if
they find out you are bright, some boys are going to be
frightened away; but they are no loss. If a boy is so insecure
that he can only be at ease with a girl who is notably less

intelligent, he is hardly a prize to be sought after. The only kind of husband you will be happy with will be one who will admire you more for your intelligence. If you have to go through life pretending that you don't know very much, you are going to be very miserable and probably a bit of a witch.

In her delightful book *Women in Wonderland*, Dorothy Dohen tells the story of a girl who was on her first date with a young man who discovered that he could not find the key to start his car on the way home and spent a half-hour searching in the gravel of the parking lot, while the girl sat quietly in the car, afraid to tell him that it was in the ignition for fear it would embarrass him. After they had been married for nine years, she was asked by a friend what she would do if the same thing happened again. "Oh, that's easy," was the reply, "I'd scream at him, 'You damn fool! it's in the ignition where you put it.'" Even though I am sure the good wife was joking, I trust it would not be out of place to suggest that both approaches left something to be desired.

I would not claim, Nancy, that a girl can get away with being rude or overbearing or snobbish in her intelligence. Such conduct would be just as inexcusable in her as in a man. Authentic intellectual humility is a requirement of humanity and not just of femininity, though I hope I will not be accused of a double standard when I say that its lack is more unfortunate in a woman than in a man. I suppose the reason is that one expects women to be more charming than men and intellectual pride and charm simply cannot coexist. However, charm is one thing and the "beautiful but dumb" act is something quite different. The smart girl is not one who hides her intelligence, but rather combines her charm and her intelligence in such fashion that she is irresistible to the kind of man who deserves her—which is to say the kind of man who respects and values what she has to offer. As for the others, forget them, they are not worth worrying about.

Intelligence then is necessary for you, Nancy, if you are to be yourself and if you are to be happily married; and by intelligence I do not mean merely the natural ability that you clearly have, but also the perfection of that ability which will come only through rigorous exercise and discipline. College will help you do that, of course, but college won't do it by itself. Indeed, it will only be the beginning of your intellectual training. You must not be like the girl who slammed her textbook on the last day of college and announced, "That's the last book I'll ever read." Nor must you be like the countless college graduates who do not in fact ever read after graduation, even if they are not quite so blunt about it. (I have been conducting a little poll among the married college graduates whom I knew while they were growing up in the Hills to see how many of them have read a book in the last year. So far I have been more successful than Diogenes—I have found one.) With the intellect one never stands still; one goes either forward or backward, and I fear that most of your predecessors are going backwards at a notable pace.

In addition it seems to me that the perfection of your intellectual abilities is required for fidelity to your Vision.

If the Vision is to have any importance in your life, you must be professionally competent; you must be good at whatever your career training is. So many girls figure that since they are going to get married there is no point in worrying about occupational skill. This is absurd; the very nature of our vocation as Christians demands that we be good at whatever we are doing, even if we are only going to do it for a short time. The mediocre apostle, the well-meaning layman who confuses enthusiasm with competence, is the worst thing that can happen to the Church, because he makes it look very foolish. Even apart from these motives, professional skill is important for a woman. She may need it if for one reason or another her husband is unable to support the family. Perhaps as the years go on, she will find it wise or necessary to engage in some part-time work. The old emphasis in Catholic marriage education against working is being drastically revised, as it becomes obvious that some women become better wives and mothers if they do some professional work each week. Surely the Catholic school systems would not be able to survive, if it were not for the mothers whose children are old enough (over sixth grade in Chicago) to enable them to teach. The school authorities say that these women who combine the skills of a teacher with the wisdom of a mother are among the very best teachers in the system. Many of their husbands and children report that the new challenge and the new interest which comes from venturing forth from the home make these women better wives and mothers too. As the shortage of trained personnel increases in this country, more and more professions will face the necessity of making part-time employment available for wives. Surely I am not trying to make a case for all wives working part-time, but I think a case can be made for it being a good thing for many wives and probably a good thing for their families, their Church, and their country.

This would suggest that you feel the obligation to keep up your professional interests during your early years in marriage, if only by reading the professional journals and the important publications in your field. In addition to enabling you to re-enter the career world if it should be necessary or proper, it will also help you to be a better wife. Some girls seem to feel that they are going to get by on their looks and their charm, that it will take nothing else to keep their husband tied to them. They forget that one can be only interesting if one is interested. If your intellect stops working on the day your first child is born, you are shortly going to become a very dull person; and you should not be surprised if your husband finds nothing to talk to you about over the supper table.

This leads to another requisite of fidelity. You must be intellectually alive; I do not really think I need urge this on one whose mind is as keen as yours. Yet there is often a temptation for a girl to feel that she is going to get through life on other faculties than her intellect, so it is not too important to be concerned with ideas. (Some day you might take a poll among your classmates to see how many read the daily paper; my own perhaps too rigid opinion is that the girl who really takes her vocation seriously will read the *New York Times* every day, but at this point I am not going to insist on it.) The intense intellectualism of the early collegiate years is replaced by the intellectual lethargy of the marriage mania period and the virtual illiteracy of early marriage. One must develop a passion for the things of the intellect—books, music, art—early in life or one will simply forget about these things as life goes on. Your vision after all starts out as a relatively fragile thing; it must be nourished by new ideas and new perspectives in years to come. If you cut yourself off from the cultural life of the world, you have ceased to be human. Like all the other requisites of fidelity which seem at first to conflict with the role of wife and mother, intellectual awareness and interest turns out under closer examination to be essential for the vocation of the culture bearer of the family. This is one of the reasons you went to college; a girl can always learn how to cook (though clearly the sooner the better); she cannot always learn how to think. If one must choose between a wife and mother who can cook and one who can think, the choice will always be for the latter because she will do a better job (though do not force your husband to choose).

I will confess, Nancy, that I am appalled by the dreadful intellectual and cultural superficiality in our community. One might excuse it among the younger males on the grounds that they have to earn a living and don't have time to devote to the finer things in life (though, as you are undoubtedly aware, I find such an argument much less than persuasive). However, what excuse do girls have? Yet they have never been to the Art Institute (unless forced to by a course in school), do not know that there is an Orchestra Hall (though more recently some of them have been there to hear the Clancy Brothers), and can proudly talk about the opera they saw (the only one, of course; you can't be a fanatic about that sort of thing). The high point of their cultural lives is a reserved seat movie and an occasional summer pilgrimage to Ravinia—for a "pops" concert, of course. If this is our emerging lay aristocracy, we are in a bad way indeed.

There is a spiritual element in the picture too. We tend to consider our prayers to be our "spiritual" life and our cultural and intellectual life to be something entirely different—as though it were one part of the soul which prayed and another part which thought and perceived the beautiful. Actually the dichotomy is a false one. The intellect is the spark of the divine in us and when it seeks its object—truth —it is also seeking Him who is Truth. Contemplation is the consideration of truth which ought—all other things being equal—to lead us to Truth. Interest in the things of the intellect is no substitute for prayer nor even necessarily a guarantee that we will pray. But it ought normally to enrich our prayer, to create a climate in which it is easier to pray, and to add greater depth to what we pray about. The more human we are the better we are able to relate to our Creator; and we cannot be human if we neglect our specifically human faculty. God can be in contact, through special grace, with a non-intellectual, but it is difficult, indeed, for Him to be in contact with an anti-intellectual, with one who denies the importance of that very faculty which distinguishes man from the beast.

I think we are going to spend our next YCS session on

the "educated woman," though I don't know how the moderators will break the subject down so the teenagers will know what we are talking about. I'll let you know the results if anything interesting comes up. By the way, the moderators' group is prospering as never before. I think we have at last found a formula that works.

God bless,

The Questing Mind

Dear Nancy,

The YCS moderators' meeting on the education of women turned out amazingly well. I was quite surprised at the consensus which existed in the group; apparently the forces of liberal education are rising again. Damien summed up the feeling of the group by saying, "Girls ought to go to college for the same reason boys go—to develop their minds." John Henry Newman rides again. However, before we get swept off our feet by optimism, let us also note that the group did not think that such a view was especially common in the college world today. Our studies at NORC would lead us to suspect that it might be more common than a lot of people think, but there doesn't seem to be any reason to suggest that anti-intellectualism has been routed just yet.

In her book, *The Feminine Mystique*, Betty Friedan has some priceless quotes from college girls, which, even though they are selected to fit her theory, are nonetheless hardly untypical of the way a lot of your contemporaries think.

One girl commented about intellectual interests, "Girls don't get excited about things like that any more. We don't

93

want careers. Our parents expect us to go to college. Everybody does. You're a social outcast at home if you don't. But
a girl who got serious about anything she studied . . . would
be peculiar, unfeminine. I guess everybody wants to graduate
with a diamond ring on her finger. That's the important
thing."

Another one denied that there was anything in the way
of serious intellectual conversation among her friends, "We
never waste time like that. We don't have bull sessions about
abstract things. Mostly we talk about our dates. Anyhow I
spend three days a week off campus. There's a boy I'm interested in. I want to be with him." And yet another was of
the opinion that, "If your husband is an organization man
you can't be too educated. The wife is awfully important for
the husband's career. You can't be too interested in art or
something like that." (She should tell this to Mrs. Kennedy.)
And a girl who had dropped out of the honors course ad-
mitted, "The other way was harder and more exciting. I
don't know why I stopped, maybe I just lost courage." A
similar comment from a senior, "suddenly you wish you'd
read more, talked more, taken the hard courses you skipped.
So you'd know what you're interested in. But I guess those
things don't matter when you're married."*

Now I have learned enough sociology to be aware that
a handful of quotes do not a theory prove, yet I don't think
I have to produce any statistical tables, Nancy, to convince
you that such an attitude is not limited merely to the colleges
Mrs. Friedan visited. I would suspect that you have heard

* These comments are cited in Friedan, *op. cit.*, pp. 151-155.

variations of those quotations almost every day from your classmates and so has every other college girl in the country. Such an attitude is not typical of everyone of course, but it must often seem that those who feel differently are swimming against the current.

Harold Taylor, one of America's greatest educators, observes that there are three kinds of female college graduates. The first he calls the co-ed (though I do not think that she is altogether absent from Catholic girls' colleges either). Says Taylor,

She is a sorority girl; educated for the most part, outside the classroom. While in college she is in open competition for eligible bachelors and measures her success . . . by the number of men who ask the pleasure of her company to go to dances, to drink Coca Colas, to have lunch or to go on picnics. She is gay, happy, extroverted, attractive, healthy, very active, restless, anxious to be doing what everybody else is doing and very anxious about perhaps being left behind. Her intellectual life can only be said to be underdeveloped and her social life is the main aspect of her college career. College for her is a continuation of high school.

Does she sound like anyone we know, Nancy?

The second group we perhaps know a little less well, since they are more the product of eastern Protestant aristocracy than of middle western Irish Catholic new rich. This is the kind of girl who reads the right books, moves in the right social circles and thinks the right thoughts, "She raises a family, helps her husband . . . spends her time in women's clubs, at forums about women, in circulating libraries, in garden clubs, beauty parlors, dog kennels, and amateur theatricals." Unfortunately they are going through the motions and really do not know what they are doing or what they are talking about.

They are, within a limited parochial framework, intelligent, educated women, but they are seeing and commenting on things which they simply do not understand. The areas of their experience as women have been close and narrow. They fail to understand the social origins of their own particular place in American society. They have no idea of the things which go on in American society which make it possible for them to exist at all. This is the source of their immaturity continued into the age of fifty-five, so that they remain sophomores in most of the important aspects of their lives.

As I said, Nancy, we have not quite got to that stage yet here in the Hills, but unless I am mistaken I can see it beginning to emerge. It takes the New Rich about a generation to turn into an aristocracy and to make the transition from the cocktail over the bridge table to the dog kennel. You will hold me excused from judging which is worse.

Taylor's description of the third kind is so excellent that I must quote every word of it,

The person of the third type is the person who, through her education, has learned how to live more fully. This college woman makes up her own mind about ideas, books, people, her children, the school board, politicians, and husbands. She is careful about whom she marries. She may be boisterous or shy, pretty or plain, lonely or gregarious, introverted or extroverted, a dancer or a scholar, a housewife or a doctor or something of each, and she may know a great deal about science or about poetry [or even, Nancy, about philosophy]. She may like skiing [Ugh] or knitting but she has a sense that her life and her education are something to be enjoyed, and to be used, and something to which she can give commitments and loyalties. She has been educated not in subjects, not in a body of knowledge, not in a standard text, but she has been educated to develop a sensitive and flexible mind, and a way of facing reality, whether it is the reality of home and children or the reality of a profession, with a trust in herself and a respect for the necessities. This means that she does what she has to do with grace and what she wants to do with pleasure.

When the problem of deciding between a home and a career emerges, she does not blame her college for having made her interested in a career or in literature or in science, or in poetry. She does not blame her husband for having presented her with children. She may spend a modest amount of time in her own interests. She may have a part-time job; she may write or do stenography, or paint or sculpt, but whatever she does, she has learned to organize her own life, whatever that involves, and she has learned to do it with a degree of maturity and self-reliance.

That describes it just about perfectly; and we can complete the picture for the Catholic by adding the words of Cardinal Newman, "I want a laity, not arrogant, nor rash in speech, not disputatious; but men [and I am sure he would mean women, too] who know their religion, who enter into it, who know just where they stand, who know what they believe and what they do not, who know their creed so well that they can give an account of it, who know so much of history that they can defend it. I want an intelligent, well-instructed laity."*

* John Henry Newman, *The Idea of a University.*

If we combine Taylor and Newman and say that this combination represents a description of what the Church ought to expect from its college educated women, I fear that we must confess that we are not getting very many— nor for that matter are there many men who measure up to comparable standards. I am not inclined to put all the blame on the colleges either, but the fact remains that a great many girls are going through the motions of four years of higher education with nothing much to show for the experience besides a diamond ring, a somewhat better vocabulary, and a more sophisticated manner with a cigarette.

I presume that you realize I am not equating the desired effects of college education with good marks. It ought to be clear by now that a girl can go through college with a straight A and still not be educated. Since they tend in our society to be more methodical and conscientious than boys, girls get better marks. They take copious notes and study hard for tests. Indeed, when one lectures at a girls' college, he finds that he is speaking to a mass of hair-do's, since the faces that go with the hair are bent over notebooks. (One professor decided to see whether he could get any reaction from a dull class and announced to the young ladies, "Western Civilization is coming to an end." Immediately this fact was noted in twenty-three notebooks and the pencils remained poised for further words to be transcribed.) There is nothing wrong with good marks, certainly, and a student —male or female—ought to try to do well in classroom work. However, as I have said so often at our meetings, we must not let studies interfere with our education, nor must we identify the two. For girls the danger is especially serious, since a girl can persuade herself that since she has done well in her studies, she need not worry about education.

Who then is the educated woman? I think Harold Taylor has described her perfectly,

The purposes of colleges for women is not to train housewives or child technicians, or professional wives, but to develop women who are emotionally and intellectually mature, and who are interesting to themselves, and to other people. These are the women who are the wisest mothers, the best wives, and the most responsible citizens. . . . I am not suggesting that colleges should ignore the fact that women will be looking after homes and bringing up children. What I mean to say is, that the kind of wife and mother who will make the greatest contribution both to society and to her children, to herself and to the country in which she lives— that kind of person is the one who has learned how to use her intelligence and her personal talents in the service of other people and in the enrichment of her own life.

I am not maintaining that you cannot be a good mother without a college education or even that a college education necessarily makes one a human being. Clearly such a position would be absurd. Humanity can develop outside of college and it can be squelched in college. However, I think there is a vast difference between not going to college because one cannot go and not going when one can go—or, equivalently, going to college and not getting anything out of it. If one cannot go to college, then there will be other ways of developing one's personality, since not going does not involve a No to possibilities of personal expansion. However, wasting an opportunity is a very different matter. It is not merely the absence of something, but it is rather the deliberate refusal of a possibility of growth. It is the act of refusing which stunts the personality far more than merely missing something which would be helpful. The girl who wastes her college education is far less human than the one who could not go.

There may be times when it will seem to you that your education was wasted; such times of discouragement, Nancy, are inevitable but don't let them mislead you. As one mother put it,

In hours of despair when I was a young mother, I regretted the years I'd spent in learning to use my mind when, I thought, I should have been learning to use my hands. By the time my children were of school age, I regretted that I did not have an M.A. or a Ph.D. as well as a B.A. I had by trial and error acquired sufficient domestic skill, but I could never hope to acquire the background of general information in the sciences and the arts every mother of mentally alert children needs. A liberal arts education, I realized then, is of more value to a woman in the day-to-day rearing of her children than it is to many a man in business. Never too high for her, it was ever too narrow.*

Well, I don't know whether you will ever want an M.A. or a Ph.D., but I know a pretty good sociology department at a rather prominent middle western university that . . . .

In the things I have been saying (and quoting), there is a danger of a serious misunderstanding. You might get the idea that the main purpose of education is that a woman

* Quoted in Dohen, *op. cit.*, pp. 239-240.

become "interesting," that she be able to look good in intellectual conversation, that her husband will be proud of his wife's glittering intelligence. I think that such a temptation might be very subtle, since it sounds at first blush rather like the standard notions of what a liberal education is for. Dorothy Dohen gets at the root of the problem:

Many people who would scorn studying simply for a degree still acquire an education exclusively for its external effect, perhaps not for its purely monetary value, but for its social, companionable value. Or, at least, whether intended or not, that seems to be the result. One is well-read and keeps the conversation going. One can make endless, apt quotations; one has an opinion on Dylan Thomas and can take either side with ease if there is a debate on the Catholicity of Graham Greene. Conversation is a fine and important thing, but there is the danger that conversational gambits can become merely goods to be displayed. What have these goods done to oneself? Do they help at all when one is alone? Do they deepen, sharpen one's thought, or even give one something to think about? Do they give significance to the ordinary duties one performs? Give a heightened awareness of the reality behind the trivialities of every day? (The breeze rustling the paper, the child's light laughter.) The woman who has studied as literature the Bible, Dante, Chaucer, Bernanos—should she not somehow see the symbolism of the objects involved in her housewifeliness, of bread and meat, water and soap, more than her less educated neighbor? And if she does not, cannot, why?*

So let's be perfectly clear about it, Nancy; you are not going to college to be a brilliant conversationalist (you were

* *Ibid.*, pp. 246-247.

that before you went). If you don't come out of college something of a contemplative—at least in the sense that Dorothy Dohen was describing—then you have been wasting your time. The situation is actually quite simple:

In closing off experience from ourselves (and I do not mean the experience of earning money or entering a profession—which is a separate problem—but simply the experience of exploiting one's imaginative faculties) they close themselves off both from men and from children. By courting a diversity of experience, on the other hand, they allow the fundamental womanly attributes— maternalism, responsiveness, and compassion—to flourish over a larger terrain. . . . Why should we believe that intellectuality means a sacrifice of feminine graces or that the graces thrive less abundantly when a woman's mind is being exercised than when it stagnates?*

A lot of quotations in this letter, Nancy, and not by accident either. I hope I have shown that what I have been talking about in the last few letters are not merely the manic ravings of someone isolated in an ivory rectory on Hamilton Avenue. I sometimes get the impression, when I make a statement which seems to me to be self-evident, that the young people of the Hills look at me as though I were going through another period of dementia, or even worse that they suspect that I am some kind of wild Bolshevik. So far have we come that the best in the Western tradition of liberal education sounds radical, when actually it is conservative in the best sense of the word. But if I am indeed insane, let

* Diana Trilling, "Are Women's Colleges Really Necessary?" *Women Today*, ed. E. Bragdon (New York: Bobbs-Merrill, 1953), p. 270.

it at least be clear that it is an insanity which is shared by the best minds that Western civilization has produced. Damien is right: "Girls ought to go to college for the same reasons boys go—to develop their minds." Any other theory, no matter how popular it might be, is absolute nonsense.

God bless,

Theory and Abstraction

Dear Nancy,

If Lent comes, Easter is only six weeks away, so it should not be too long before the clans assemble once again. That ought to be a cheerful thought, I guess, but I have begun to dread vacations because each one seems to mark a more obvious deterioration of happiness. Sometimes I just can't believe that people can survive the level of unhappiness they generate for themselves. Well, survive they do and they are not going to change, so there's no point worrying too much about them.

To your letter—I am not sure whether the education of a girl ought to be very different from that of a boy. George Shuster, the former president of Hunter College and surely one of the most charming and shrewd observers of American education, writes in his memoirs that, "you ought not to educate a woman as if she were a man or to educate her as if she were not."* Now that clearly sounds like a contradiction, but I don't think it is. My hunch is that Dr. Shuster is

* George N. Shuster, *The Ground I Walked On* (New York: Farrar, Straus, 1961), p. 3.

saying that the problems in the education of a girl are different than those in the education of a boy, but that the different problems cannot be solved by different educational methods.

I would think that the purpose of educating a girl is in part to add a masculine element to her thought processes, just as the purpose of educating a boy is, in part, to add a feminine element to his thought processes. In our culture at least there is a considerable amount of evidence, both scientific and impressionistic, that men have a flair for abstract and theoretical thought, while women are especially good at the concrete and practical (whether this difference is cultural or biological is an interesting question, but one that hardly need detain us at this point). A liberal education should enable a girl to develop those kinds of thought processes to which her cultural position would not normally incline her; in the same fashion, it should help a boy to develop habits of thought which his role in society would not normally demand of him. Thus a girl in addition to enriching and developing her mastery of the concrete should also do battle with the long-range and the theoretical, and the boy in addition to improving his analytical abilities should develop some skills in intuitive knowledge, especially, for example, from a study of art, music, and poetry.

Jacques Barzun agrees with me (note the order) on this subject (and this is positively the last long quote for the rest of the year):

It is true that as a general rule, girls are less interested than boys in theory, in ideas, in the logic of things and events. That is why their minds must not be cluttered up with details they instinctively prefer—and make no use of. Girls are more conscientious and hard-working, they want to please their teachers more, and they do not want to be bothered by implications. They argue less and the art of winning which they have been taught since the cradle has given them a respect for convention which makes them unerringly pick out the accepted hokum. At the same time they are practical enough to distrust it, and the distrust ends by tainting all intellectual matters, so that one constantly meets women of fine intelligence who use their brains exclusively about concrete things such as clothes, food, and the persons whom they know. Their imagination about the distant or the abstract has completely atrophied; they are at the mercy of words, and their vehement opinions about war or strikes or politics are little short of brutism. Though it may be hard work, the minds of women students can be forced out of their groove of conventionality and made to cope even with abstractions.*

I said no more long quotations but while I was copying that one out I remembered similar words from Edith Stein:

The personal tendency is usually unwholesomely exaggerated; on the one hand woman is inclined to be extravagantly concerned with her own person and to expect the same interest from others; this expresses itself in vanity, desire for praise, and recognition and an unrestrained urge for self-expression and communication. On the other hand we shall find an unmeasured interest in others which shows itself as curiosity, gossip and an indiscreet longing to penetrate into the intimate life of other people. The tendency towards wholeness easily leads her to frittering away her energy, it makes her disinclined to discipline her individual talents properly and leads to superficial nibbling in all directions. In her

---

* Jacques Barzun, *Teacher in America* (Boston: Little, 1945); citation taken from paperback edition (New York: Doubleday, 1954), p. 219.

attitude towards others it shows itself in a possessiveness far exceeding what is required by her maternal functions. Thus the sympathetic companion becomes the interfering busybody that cannot tolerate silent growth and thus does not foster development but hinders it.*

Now this last quote may sound like grist for the mill of certain young men from our happy neighborhood who have insisted all along that this was the way girls are. You will note therefore that Edith Stein was a woman—and indeed one of the most remarkable women of our time.

I am not an educator, Nancy, much less an educator of women (my one class a week at UC doesn't count), so I am in no position to say how educators ought to proceed in facing this problem of a woman's inclination for the concrete and the particular. However, I do feel that the individual girl can be aware of this tendency and strive to counter-balance it. I do not say that she should try to stop thinking as women in our culture think, but I do say that she should also seek to develop her intellect by trying at times to think like a man.

Perhaps in your case this is less of a problem than it would be for others, since you do display on occasion a considerable capacity for abstract and logical thought. However, I trust you will not be angry with me if I say that, as with so many other girls, this skill at masculine thought patterns is not always predictable. It seems to me at times that girls like you occasionally become very frightened of what they

*Stein, *op. cit.*

discover when they indulge in abstract thinking and quickly return to the emotional and the concrete. Also your writing, which is very good, tends to be impressionistic and "short run"; I would not want you to eliminate the vivid sense of the real which your writing displays, but I think it might be enriched by a bit more of the perspective and depth that abstraction can provide.

Let me add that I think too much is made of the differences between the way men think and the way women think. It is clear enough that each has different tendencies, and that at times they will be at cross purposes because their approach to a given situation may well be very different. Nevertheless, over the long haul, there can be no doubt that their native abilities are remarkably similar and there is no reason to think that one is more intelligent than the other (certain mutual friends of ours to the contrary notwithstanding). I have a large hunch that the differences we see result in great part from the fact that the social roles of each permit them to let certain parts of their intellectual equipment atrophy, and that a truly liberal education will substantially decrease the difference in thinking between a man and woman as it enables them to rise above their social role. Accordingly, a liberally educated husband and wife should have less trouble understanding each other than will people who are not so educated (all other things—including personality—being equal). So I guess you can make a case that liberal education makes for a happy home life.

Of course, the differences in intellectual approaches are not going to vanish, since they are rooted in social and ultimately in biological roles. Nor would we want to see them vanish, because in their own way they are as important as the biological differences. But, while we certainly want the happy differences to remain, we want them to remain in a disciplined fashion—and for a girl this would apparently require a strenuous effort to take the long-range view and to think theoretically, at least on as many occasions as possible.

How can this be done in practice? Well, I feel rather foolish trying to tell a philosophy major that she ought to think abstractly. By definition there is nothing quite as good as metaphysics for getting one out of the concrete, although I suppose that math might also serve the same purpose. My own personal prejudice is in favor of the social sciences which, when studied properly, are thoroughly "liberal" studies because they enable us to rise above the prejudices of our society, our culture, and our personality. There is no doubt about it: because we are well-to-do Irish Catholics from the South Side of Chicago, we think in certain definite patterns which make it very difficult to understand, for example, Negroes who live but ten minutes away from us. Sociology may not really enable us to get inside of the mentality of other people and reason the way they do, but it at least will make us think twice before we condemn others because their values and goals are different from ours. We will have come to understand that social class is an extraordinarily powerful force in shaping the human being, and that unless we take it into account we will never understand others who are even slightly different from us.

Another exercise which is extremely helpful for a girl is

to try to do some long-range planning. If we think of some of the projects that The Organization tackled last summer, we can remember that the girls were remarkably good at the day-by-day things, like running the remedial reading school or organizing a dance, but that when it came to long-range things, like the study week at the end of the summer or the future of our work among the young people of the parish, the distaff side had little to offer, or indeed even little inclination to think about such things. I would suggest that, even though it might involve considerable effort, the girls ought to strive to think in terms of next year or the next ten years, instead of abdicating their responsibility for anything that does not occur the day after tomorrow. You are surely aware of what happens when this does not happen; we have seen too many all-girl projects fold because no one had any idea of where the work was going, and no one had done any planning for alternative procedures if a situation should change.

Another way to train oneself in abstract thought would be to force yourself to become interested in politics, world affairs, contemporary problems. I wasn't just joking when I said you ought to be reading the *New York Times* every day. You should not become like a good number of women I know who never get beyond the "women's section" (i.e., recipes, fashions, advice to the lovelorn and society gossip) or the death notices (the so-called Irish sports section) of the daily paper. Nor should your goal be to have an opinion when some boy asks what you think of the Kerr Bill (as did one odd type last summer of every girl he encountered). These are important areas of human activity and anyone who is human must be concerned with them; that the humanity is modified by femininity does not change the obligation—not even if most women think it does.

I am frankly appalled by the ignorance of many of the young people in our neighborhood (male as well as female) on these subjects. I remember one crack Fr. H. made at Christmas time to a room full of people that alluded to something the President had said at his press conference (about the *First Family* album) and had been on the front page of all four Chicago papers. Not a girl in the room caught it. They'll get to be real good at the death notices though. I will admit, Nancy, that you will find it difficult to cultivate such interests, but, if it is any consolation, it will be no more difficult than it is for the average boy to learn to sit still through a concert or walk around a museum.

This has been a pretty funny letter, even though it may not seem so. Like a typical male, I have made a marvelous theoretical and abstract argument that women should try to think more theoretically and abstractly. For concrete arguments on this subject, I refer you to some good nun.

God bless,

Direct Involvement

Dear Nancy,

I have the hardest time persuading people that I am not really a pessimist. Everyone goes around muttering about what a grim and discouraged kind of fellow I am. It's simply not true. It may come as a shock to you, but the theological underpinnings of these letters (insofar as they have any) are solidly optimistic. With Father Teilhard, I am convinced that the divine milieu is more obvious today than at any time in history; and with Father Hans Küng, I would argue that this is the greatest epoch that the Church has ever known. Indeed, the pace of change within the Church and the possibilities for influence on the world beyond the Church seem to me to be quite breathtaking. Things are much better today than would have seemed possible even ten years ago, indeed, even a year before the first session of the Council. I don't see how anyone who looks at the Church Universal and the Church American today can help but be dizzily optimistic.

So you can imagine my surprise when people, especially from the Cana and Christian Family Movements, ask me why I am so pessimistic. They apparently equate dissatisfaction over our slowness to respond to the possibilities of the present situation with pessimism; actually, of course, my dissatisfaction flows from long-range optimism and is really much more optimistic than their approach to reality.

All of which is a somewhat lengthy introduction to a warning about two popular contemporary heresies to which you are going to be exposed (and by heresy I don't mean doctrinal error). The first one is what I would call the ghetto mentality (and occasionally in moments of spite I rather unfairly refer to it as the Cana Syndrome). Now the "Catholic ghetto" approach to American culture has received such a terrific drubbing in recent years that it has become distinctly unpopular. Indeed, it is hardly possible to read any serious article or book about the Church in America that doesn't take a poke at the "ghetto" mentality, which feels that Catholics should isolate themselves from their fellow Americans. Yet, within the family movements, there has been a tendency for a good number of people to pursue a policy which is equivalent to the "ghetto" one, without actually using the word.

The attitude I have in mind, Nancy, is one that you might have encountered often in school too. It claims that the values on family problems of most Americans are so different from the values of Catholics that the main task of the Catholic family is to preserve itself from corruption by the values of the larger society. We must be careful or *they* will ruin us or our children with their ideas. Carried to its logical extreme—as it is by an occasional family—this notion produces children who not only cannot relate to the non-

Catholics they encounter, but cannot even establish any friendships with their fellow Catholics. They are so impressed with the need to be different that they stay away from everyone else, because virtually everyone else has already been corrupted.

Now I am prepared to admit that the values of many other Americans in regard to sex, marriage, birth control, divorce and such like are at odds with Catholic values. I am further prepared to concede that we must exercise some care to see that we do not betray our own principles. However, I do not think that once we have made these two statements we have exhausted the matter. If this were all that could be said, it would be a dreadful posture for the universal Church —huddling behind its ghetto walls for fear that its members might be contaminated by the world around them. We must be secure in our own position indeed, but then we must proceed to change the world; and if the Vision about which I have talked so much means anything, it means that.

The other day I was talking to a very fine Catholic layman who was claiming that the more he looked around and saw how confused and sick the world is, the more he became convinced that the only thing for Catholic parents to do was to protect their families from being contaminated by the world. I will confess I hit the ceiling. The world may be corrupt, but it is also redeemable, and we are the ones who are to redeem it. The world is looking for Life and we are the ones who have the Life to offer it. We will never bring it redemption and life if we become spiritual cowards, afraid to associate with our fellow human beings. I don't mean that we must engage in propaganda, in the "hard sell," high pressure approach to the apostolate. I rather have in mind the immortal words of the late Cardinal Suhard, "Bearing witness to Christ means living one's life in such a way that one would be a fool if Christ were not the son of God." You can't do that hiding in a ghetto or under a bushel; you can only do it standing on the mountain top.

Nor is the contemporary world all that bad; in some areas of human morality there has been an obvious deterioration, yet as Father Fichter has insisted many times, in other areas there has been great progress. Surely we are much more conscious of the unity of the human race and of our obligation to our fellowmen "even to the ends of the earth." Again there seems to be an increasing respect in American society for the value of the human person—especially if he has been born. Nor is the new democratic, partnership approach to the use of authority in the family necessarily bad. It would be wrong, of course, for the father to abdicate his authority, but even if the democratic family is merely one in which the father ceases to be a tyrant and becomes a constitutional monarch, then I for one think it represents a substantial improvement over the domestic autocracy of the past. The world is changing very rapidly, some of the changes are for the better and some are for the worse, but there is hardly any convincing reason to say that Christianity should retreat to the foxholes; nor does the Pope who called the Second Vatican seem to think so either. "The Church of Christ— light of the World"—this is what Cardinal Suenens says is to be the goal of the Council. Hardly a ghetto approach to the world.

This is a kind of a round-about way, Nancy, of getting to the major point I want to make in this letter. Your Vision requires that you be what the French call *engagé* (this does not mean engaged, by the way, it means committed). Since you are the Church you must be concerned about whatever the Church is concerned; wherever there is misery or suffering or ignorance in the world, you must be, at least in spirit. At different times in your life cycle, you will be able to do more in the apostolate of direct personal charity than at other times; but you must always be doing something, even if it is for the time rather small. And you must be involved in prayer and in concern with whatever the Church is doing, whether it be a mission in India or racial justice in the city. These are not someone else's problems, they are your problems; and pretending that they are not is not going to do you any good.

What precisely must you do? This is something that you must figure out for yourself, no one else can tell you. Your work during the past three or four summers in the mission parishes around Chicago left little doubt as to your ability in such work. Perhaps after graduation you will want to put some time in the Peace Corps or the Papal Volunteers or the Extension Home Missionaries. Or maybe you will be able to help our own Chicago lay mission program, which by that time ought to be going strong. I am sure that these kinds of experiences would tremendously enrich the remaining years of your life, and that you would never regret them. Of course, if you are going to get married immediately after graduation, these plans become less feasible. Some people are called to such work, I guess, and others are not; but everyone is called to be a missionary. As Father Sullivan of the Extension Volunteers points out, "every parish in the country is a home mission."

One social problem that you will not be able to escape from, as long as you live in a large metropolitan region, is the race question. It is as twisted and complicated a problem as we have ever faced in America and there are no solutions on the horizon. I hardly need talk you out of race prejudice, but I think I ought to emphasize that no Christian can have an easy conscience until the terrible injustice of segregation is blotted out of our society. And neither can he remain at peace as long as there is a bit of prejudice in his own heart. There are all kinds of things wrong with the conduct of American Negroes (resulting from the way they have been treated by American whites), and at times we are very properly afraid of some of them, but we must no more judge the race by some of its members than we would want our own ethnic group judged by its alcoholics (of which there are more than a few). Nor can we be satisfied with the stereotypes and clichés, with the fears and hatred of the generation which has gone ahead of us. We must think through this problem ourselves and find out what positive action lies in our power and then take that action. Anything less is unworthy of a Christian.

I might point out, incidentally, that your work in the mission parishes means that you know more about Negroes than do most of the people in our parish. You probably don't realize it, but compared to the massive ignorance of most white people, you are an "expert" on the race question. This does not mean that older people are going to listen to you quite yet, but some day they may have to.

Besides race, what other things ought you to be interested in, especially during those busy years when you will be a mother of a young family? I think that certain kinds of interest are "naturals" for the woman of a family. First of all, the problems of the educational system are obviously in the mother's domain. By the time you have children in school, the voice of the laity will be of much more importance in Catholic education than it is today. If school administrators are to be protected from busybodies, cranks and crackpots, there will have to be some mothers in the community who are eager to make a positive and constructive contribution to the solution of the problems involved in the relationship between home and school, mothers who will not be afraid to criticize and to demand the best, but who will not be the kind who are using criticism as an outlet for the frustrations of their own neurotic personality. Of course, you will be able to make such a contribution only if you have studied the problems of education enough to know what you are talking about. If you haven't, you will rapidly become a self-constituted expert who thinks she has all the answers, when she doesn't even know what the questions are, a type which seems to have a special affinity for parent-teacher groups.

I would also think that the problems of local government, problems of efficiency and corruption, are the kind of thing about which the mother of the family would want to be well informed, since they affect the community in which she will raise her children. Nor are these problems solved when one moves out of the city into one of the clean new suburbs; the harsh fact is that in our area at least the central city is much more honestly and efficiently run than are most of the suburbs. If there is anything harder to catch than a big crook, it is a little crook. But unless you understand how society operates and how political, moral and social problems are combined, you won't know what is going on in your community or what can be done about it. In this kind of work, by the way, the League of Women Voters does a splendid job.

Again in the area of community culture you ought to be able to put your talents to good use—community theatre, children's theatre, adult education, concerts, children's drawing and sculpture classes, forums on architecture, town planning, community housing, politics, and countless other things of this kind are the proper interest of a wife and mother.

Nor can you overlook the problems of world peace and the cold war and the influence of the cold war on the life of your family and your country. We must resist the temptation to let the continuing crisis turn us into a nation of fearful, tense and suspicious people, because if this happens we will lose the very freedoms we are trying to defend. To quote Harold Taylor, "The contribution which women can make is not to create a nation of bristling, aggressive, extroverted, success-minded females all bent on mobilizing themselves for any emergency. We have all met that kind of girl. But what we need is an increase in civic sanity, and in the kind of insight and understanding which women can bring to the problems of human relations." Women must in a time of permanent crisis exercise a liberalizing and civilizing influence on a nation in arms. I wonder how many did at the time of the Cuban crisis; I wonder, indeed, how many had the faintest idea of what the crisis was all about.

You will note that none of these things are specifically Catholic; even the interest in education ought to go beyond the Catholic schools, since the other schools in the community are your schools too. You—or more exactly your husband —will be paying plenty of taxes for them, so you will want to make sure that they are, to use the currently approved word, excellent. It is high time that American Catholic women become aware that ours is an ecumenical age and that they should be working not merely with their Catholic friends. And yet how many non-Catholics does the average girl in the Hills know? You are well aware of the answer: not a one.

But this is not to say that there is not much to be done within the Church by the wife and mother. In some parishes the traditional societies have taken on new life under the leadership of the younger generation. The marriage education program of Cana-type organizations is extremely important, especially in high schools. The Confraternity of Christian Doctrine is engaged in a fantastically important apostolate among the more than 50 per cent of Catholic children who are not in Catholic schools. The Christian Family Movement is America's one unique contribution to Catholic Action and has immense potential. Because I criticize it occasionally, it does not follow that I do not think it is one of the most important organizations in the Church— despite the sensitivities of certain CFM people who feel that even the slightest criticism of the movement represents opposition. Our Young Christian Students program, I think, would benefit greatly from having some young married couples in the moderators' group; I'm convinced that we will have more such programs as the years go on. Beyond the parish level, organizations like the Catholic Interracial Council, the Catholic Council on Working Life, and the Adult Education Centers will need help increasingly from lay people and especially lay women. The problem, in Chicago at least, is not that there is nothing to do, but that there is so much to choose from.

Then there are your own personal talents which may not require an organization but which can serve the Church and the community. In your case you could develop your talents as a writer without ever leaving the house, and it should be clear to you from people you know that the Catholic press is in dire need of writers who can put a subject and a predicate together in some kind of meaningful fashion.

So the ghetto heresy is wrong and so is its first cousin, the family heresy. This heresy argues that the main responsibilities of a man and woman are to be a good husband and wife and a good mother and father; that good family life is the key to a happy society, that parents should not let anything interfere with their spending as much time as possible with their children, that people in CFM cannot help but be neglecting their children since they spend so much time going to meetings, that the spirituality of married people should be based on the sacrament of matrimony, that the mother and father's place during their free time should be with the children and with each other, and that what apostolic activity married people engage in should be joint. The family heresy is "togetherness" lifted to a theological level.

You have been at the Catholic Action game long enough, Nancy, to realize how wrong this position is. If all that is required is that men and women be good spouses and good parents, the recent Popes have been terrible fools to waste their time writing the social encyclicals (and thus *Mater et Magistra* was a particular waste). If the answer to modern social problems is simply better family life, then all the social action organizations approved by the Church all over the world should never have been permitted to exist. That good family life is not all that is needed should be evident from the fact that good husbands and wives, good mothers and fathers (in the narrow sense of the words) abound in our society, and yet the conditions of the temporal order—government, work group, economic community, international organization—grow progressively more chaotic and less Christian. Good family life—as essential and necessary as it may be—is simply not enough to transform and Christianize the social order, and the evidence is all around us.

The family is certainly the basic unit of society, but it does not follow that a reform of what traditionally have been taken to be family morals is going to change the larger communities. The disappearance of divorce, for example, would by no means solve the problem of starvation in the underdeveloped countries. It is from stable happy families that zealous lay apostles are to come, but more than stability and happiness are needed. The family must also be apostolic; and unfortunately stability and happiness do not automatically produce apostolic zeal. Indeed, the absence of a large number of family members who do possess zeal and who are determined to improve the social order, makes it difficult for many families to be either stable or happy.

So, Nancy, there is much to be done; it will be an exciting world in which to live and to raise one's children; if you ignore that world you will be cheating yourself and cheating them. And let me add that to recognize the excitement that is possible in life today is the essence of optimism.

God bless,

Personality and Freedom

Dear Nancy,

As I thought about what Hans Kung said, when he spoke in Chicago, I could not escape the notion that it is really freedom I have been talking about in all these letters. Vision, fidelity, life, self—these are all aspects of freedom. The life that the Lord brought us through His Resurrection and brings us through grace frees us from the slavery of sin. Fidelity means that we have the courage to remain free. Vision is our ability to see the need for freedom in our life and in the lives of others. And the self develops only insofar as it becomes progressively more free from prejudice and ignorance and fear.

To be free, Nancy, you must know who you are. That may sound like an odd statement, but I think it's unarguable. If you really know who you are, you can never become the slave of an outside event. If you are secure in your self-evaluation you can survive any disaster, no matter how terrible. You can lose your friends, your family, your reputation, your worldly possessions, but you still have that inner core of selfhood which nothing can shake.

125

We had a remarkable demonstration of that here a few years ago. You remember when one of our friends was expelled from college, a victim of false charges fabricated by a neurotic nun. Such a scandal would have destroyed most girls I know; their education, their career, their reputation would have seemed irreparably damaged. They would have avoided their friends, withdrawn into a shell, fled from the community, and quite possibly even had a breakdown under the strain. Yet this young lady was not shaken. I'll never forget as long as I live the night she came over to the rectory to tell us what had happened. When the sorry story was finished, there was an embarrassed moment during which I did not know what to say and she did not know whether to laugh or cry; so, of course, she laughed. She knew who she was, she knew she was innocent, and she really didn't care what anyone else said or thought. She was not going to let her personality collapse under the weight of injustice, she was not going to fall apart just because most of the world around her seemed suddenly to go to pieces. She had at her command the one weapon free men always have in the face of oppression—laughter; and since her own ego was secure in the midst of the most trying of crises, she was able to laugh and hence able to survive.

It really does not matter that her friends rallied to her support, that the school was forced to reverse its stand, that the injustice was revoked. In the few harrowing weeks when her future hung in the balance, she was able to keep on laughing. As one of the men in the parish told a nun from the school, "She wasn't disgraced, but you were." People who know who they are are indestructible; this is not to say that they do not need friends or help; everyone does. But like Job they can survive crises and live for the dawn of another day.

You see what I am getting at, Nancy; "unfreedom," as Father Kung calls it, results from fear and fear in its turn results from ignorance and insecurity. If you know who you are, then you are secure, you are not afraid, you are free.

How do you get to know who you are? I wish I could answer that. I have only known a handful of young people who did know and I have no idea how they found out. Only two of them have been girls, the one I just mentioned and another. Hardly enough to fashion a generalization. A few others seem to be close to it, but whether they will really find themselves remains to be seen.

To know yourself, to find out who you are, you must certainly have the courage to be honest. By this I mean that you must not try to make everyone happy by pretending to be someone that you are not. It is hard for a girl who has always been popular to realize that it is inevitable that she will displease some people, upset others, anger yet others, and perhaps even hurt a few, if she is going to be the person she is, instead of the one they want her to be. Until this stage of her life she has been able to charm everyone without encountering any conflicts; now the necessity for honest decisions makes conflict inevitable. It is especially hard to accept the fact that no matter what the decisions are, someone is going to be hurt, but such is the effect that original sin has had on human society. The only possible answer to someone whose emotional system rebels against the thought of hurting anyone is that the hurt will only be temporary, and she is faced with the choice of inflicting small hurts now on people who will rapidly get over them, or large hurts in the future from which the victims will not recover. Lack of honesty in our relations with others merely postpones and intensifies the harm we do to them.

So you can only find out who you are by doing what you want to do. I am not preaching selfishness or lack of consideration, but I do think that you must make your own decisions and not let anyone else make them for you, whether it be by direct persuasion or by subtle pressure. It is much easier not to make your own decisions, to let other people make them and to convince yourself that you want what they want. Some people develop this art of "unfreedom" to a remarkable degree of skill. They never really decide anything for themselves and yet manage to give the impression that they are running their own lives. One of the distinct advantages of such a procedure is that it always provides you with a scapegoat. If something goes wrong there is always someone else to blame; the mistake, the error in judgment, is always in the external environment and not in the self. Only the free man is strong enough to admit that he made a mistake.

I suspect that there is a bit of stubbornness implied in finding out who you are, an unwillingness to swallow the advice of the "conventional wisdom," a refusal to admit that others know more about what is good for you than you do yourself, a determination to look people straight in the eye and if necessary say, "You're wrong." You ought not to be obnoxious about your independence, especially since a nine-teen-year-old girl really does not have too much experience on which to base her decisions; but the only way she is going to acquire the experience is by making her own mistakes. Stubbornness and humility can co-exist. Your attitude ought to be, "Look, I may very well be all wrong, but if I am wrong then I will learn from it, much more than if you are right and I do what you want me to do." You should not try to be so independent that you do not listen to the advice of others or carefully weigh what they have to say. Independence does not mean rudeness or imprudence; it does not mean that you think that the older generation has absolutely nothing important to say—even though some young people act as if this were the case. But it does mean that young people realize that unless they start making their own decisions, after carefully pondering all that others have said, they will never become adults.

Another way to get to know who you are is to get to know other people. During the teens it is difficult to really know your friends, because you are so dependent on them. They are an essential part of the environment, but despite all the spilling of secrets and the exchanging of confidences, there is not very much communication between personalities; there cannot be since the high school type is so concerned with herself that she is hardly aware of the existence of someone else as a person in her own right. She may criticize the actions of others or be disappointed in what her friends do, but she is incapable of understanding what the psychological processes are at work in others, and hence totally incapable of thinking that similar processes might be operating within her own personality.

This kind of learning is insightful rather than deductive. You discover the personality of the other in the same instant that you discover your own. Hence you cannot—and clearly should not—use your friends as tools in your quest for self-knowledge. But you can strive to understand your friends better, if only so as to be a better friend. And I should note that you ought to realize that you are not the only one in the group that is growing up; hence if the group is to survive (and most adolescent groups don't), the whole system of relationships is going to have to be restructured. Even though it may theoretically seem as if it would be fun, your friendships cannot go on in the same fashion as they did when you were in high school.

The best way to get to know yourself is in prayer. I don't mean prayer of petition or even at this point the public prayer of the Mass (although this does have a role to play in our search for identity). I have in mind prayer of reflection. Now reflection is not too popular in the Hills—or indeed any neighborhood—especially among girls. It seems that people try to keep moving at a rapid pace so as to avoid the slightest possibility of there being time for thought. Nothing else to do? Get in the car and find some of the group so we can ride around together. A quiet evening or a quiet weekend? Nothing could be worse, why doesn't someone have a party? Stay home on Friday night and read a book? Good heavens, better that the world come to an end!

I am not being facetious. People in our neighborhood

(and not just young people) are afraid to be by themselves, to take time out to think. Indeed, they are temperamentally incapable even of being alone. Though they flock to retreats and days of recollection, they actually do not do much recollecting because of their irrational desire to be talking to someone else. Of course they must talk; the alternative is thought and what could be worse? Nor do I think this is an entirely unconscious mechanism. In some cases it is very deliberate; people do not want to think about their lives for fear that they will discover that their lives are being wasted. They do not want to take a long, critical look at themselves because they suspect they won't like what they see. They do not want to face up to their problems, because then the responsibility to seek a solution would be unavoidable. So they run from reflection, which is to say they run from reality and from themselves. They lose themselves in their work or their families or their social life or their bottle. It is so much more comfortable to keep one's head buried in the sand.

Even apart from its value in your prayer life, reflection is essential if you are to remain human. Chesterton once wrote an essay "On the Advantages of Doing Nothing." We must periodically do nothing; we must have done with the strange Calvinist notion which has crept into our Irish American culture, that doing nothing is a waste of time; we must escape from the heresy of action, from our compulsive desire to be on the move. Doing nothing is a highly positive kind of activity since it involves pause and reflection, the seeking of perspective and insight, the asking of embarrassing questions, and the facing of the one who should be our most rigorous critic—ourself. Such reflection is not necessarily prayer (at least in the strict sense of the word), much less is it contemplation; but it is a necessary prelude to prayer and for the man of faith it almost automatically leads to prayer. I think it is an axiom of our psychological life that if we do not have time to do nothing, then we will not have time for prayer, since honest prayer is even more destructive of our defenses and our escape mechanisms.

None of these suggestions are magic formulas for finding out who you are. The final years of the teens are perhaps the most difficult in your emotional life. In the early years of high school you were just beginning to become conscious of the problem of identity and just beginning to search for an answer. At nineteen the need for a solution has become desperate. You are on the verge of adulthood and the major decisions which being an adult involves. The identifications with various heroines of your teen years are no longer sufficient. You must have an identity or you will have no firm stand from which to make your decisions. Either you acquire this identity or your personality remains nothing more than the attitudes of the last person to whom you talked or the majority vote of the group you happen to be in. In the most literal sense of the word, you are nobody. But at nineteen it often looks as if the latter course is the easier. It is so much more comfortable and pleasant to be a nobody rather than to be someone. The rigors of the final steps of identity formation are so great that virtually every young man and young woman is tempted to run. A little bit of running may not be so very bad; the self can be rather frightening, and a good case can be made for the argument that it must be approached discreetly and carefully. He who runs from one position only so as to take up a better position to continue the quest may be simply engaging in smart strategy. The only trouble is that most people don't stop running. If you want to be happy, Nancy, you must stop running. There is no alternative.

There remains one final way of finding your identity and I have saved it for the end because it is the best way of all—the way of love. I don't mean the dizzy romanticism of the adolescent song or the adolescent crush, but I mean rather the generous service of others. As W. H. Auden put it, "The ego is but a dream until another's need by name define it." One must have the beginnings of identity before one can love; but in the final analysis it is only love which will enable you to know who you are.

God bless,

Faith in the Modern World

Dear Nancy,

A lot of nonsense has been written the last few years about the role of women in the modern world. Much of it is somewhat appalling because it is either strident or mushy, either affirming that women can do everything men can do or waxing mystical about the glories of femininity. Yet I think that there is a balance which can be struck between the two positions that does point out a contribution in the contemporary world that we are not going to be able to expect from the male half of the race.

Edith Stein goes too far in the following statement, but she makes a good point,

Woman tends towards the living and personal, she wants the whole. To cherish, to keep and protect, that is her natural, her authentically maternal desire. The dead thing, the object, interests her in the first place insofar as it serves the living and the personal rather than for its own sake. This is connected with another feature; every kind of abstraction is foreign to her nature. The living and personal which is the object of her care, is a concrete whole and must be cared for and encouraged as a whole, not one part at the expense of others. And to this practical attitude corresponds her theoretical endowment; her natural way of knowledge is not so much notional and analytical, but envisaging and sensing the concrete*

As you might remember from my earlier letters, Nancy, I think that this concrete approach to reality ought to be balanced in part by the acquisition of certain masculine thought patterns. But I would not deny that in our culture at least women tend to generate more personal warmth than do men. It is not so much that men don't love, as that man's love does not seem quite as, how should I say it, soothing and reassuring as does woman's love. If man is expected to bring order and progress into the world, then woman is expected to bring peace, confidence, calm, serenity. I would not be so naïve as to say that most women do this; but I would argue that this is the kind of contribution which Western society seems to require from the female half of the race. I think we all feel that a neurotic, anxious, compulsive woman is somehow or other more in contradiction to the demands of her role in society than is a man with the same symptoms.

Am I saying then that woman's contribution to the modern world is love? This, of course, is standard day-of-recollection and college-commencement-address material and has something to be said for it. But my own hunch is that the matter goes deeper. Love is involved in the female "role," but more importantly, I suspect, so is faith. I don't mean just supernatural faith, though I suspect girls are

* Stein, *op. cit.*

probably better at this too, but I mean trust and confidence in the ultimate goodness of creation, and confidence, further, in the ability of those whom they love to see their family, their society, their world through crises. Women must be the generators of optimism in a world which often looks pretty dismal. I guess it is almost trite to say that the faith of his woman (mother, wife, daughter) sustains many a man when he has lost faith in himself; yet this is one of the great and beautiful facets of human life, and the fact that it is a commonplace does not make it any less important.

In the final analysis, the warmth and confidence-generating ability of women is surely beyond the explanatory powers of a parish priest turned sociologist; it is the proper province of the poet, the mystic, the philosopher. But to retreat to the very limited area of truth from which we sociologists operate, I would say that to the extent that women fail in their role as the "socio-emotional" or "expressive" leaders in the family and the community, the world is going to become a rather unpleasant place. To put it in less jargonist words, Nancy, if women turn from warmth and confidence to neurotic nagging, if they lose their ability to love because they have lost their faith, then the world is going to be one very hellish part of the universe. If our highly rationalized and mechanistic society loses the bit of humanity that womenkind usually inject into life, it just possibly won't survive; nor ought it to.

On this subject we have no data, so I don't know whether women are less womanly than they used to be. I rather suspect that the world is so rationalized that it probably needs more faith and more warmth than it used to. I am not convinced that it is going to get it. Many women are looking for the wrong things in the wrong places and taking their frustrations and disappointments out on their husbands and their children. Faith becomes shrewishness, optimism becomes greed, warmth becomes neurosis, and love turns to smothering, possessive affection. Women like this (and their number is legion) are enough to persuade anyone that, even on the most natural of levels, celibacy is the only safe choice.

What has happened to these women? By now, Nancy, the answer must be getting monotonous: they have been faithful neither to themselves nor their Vision. Infidelity kills faith in the natural order just as much as in the supernatural. They settled for some simple answer, thinking that happiness came without hard work, that identity could be obtained without sacrifice, and that love could come without self-control. Their dreams did not come true and they did not have the strength to live with reality. So they have become bitter, sour, disillusioned. Everything that was womanly in them has been stifled and they are harsh, hard, and brittle. I might add that they are extremely neurotic and bigoted. Witch is perhaps too charitable a term.

Now I am not advocating, Nancy, that you turn into a bubbling bundle of sentiment. Pollyanna didn't have faith, she was blind. Sentimentality is a good thing and feminine sentimentality is one of the better things the world has to offer, but it is not very durable. The emotions of the high school sophomore are not without charm—in limited amounts

—but they don't have much to do with faith. If the emotionality of a woman is not disciplined by self-control and by
intellectual restraint, it will either turn sour or diffuse itself
in irrelevancies.

One of the measures of the maturity of a woman's
optimism is her capacity for anger. Girls are great at com-
forting people in time of suffering, but unfortunately wiping
tears away is not enough when one is faced with social
injustice. Compassion is taken to be a feminine virtue and I
am sure it is; but if compassion is content at feeling sorry for
people and not trying to root out the cause of their suffering,
then it readily becomes irrelevant. There ought to be a touch
of Joan of Arc, a touch of the warrior saint, within every
woman who takes her role in the Church seriously.

The Blessed Mother is, I should think, the ideal model
of the feminine contribution of which I have been speaking.
Unfortunately the spooks have taken over much of the
Marian devotion that teenagers encounter; Mary is viewed
as some kind of negative sex goddess, always saying "No."
One would gather from the crusades for decent dress, decent
literature and decent disks that the key Marian virtue is
chastity. Yet there is no foundation in the Bible for such an
emphasis on purity to the exclusion of all else. Indeed, the
main virtue of the Blessed Mother with which Scripture is
concerned is faith. I am convinced that perhaps the most
marvelous example of faith (in the sense I have been using
the word) the world has ever known is contained in the
remark at Cana, "Whatever He tells you to do, do it." I don't
think there is any doubt that these words show us exactly

what role Mary played in the early Church, and the role a Catholic woman should play in her family and her Church today. It would certainly be reassuring to have people like that around.

Nor is there an element of the Joan of Arc missing from the Marian image. If Mary is mother of the Church ("woman, behold thy Son"), she would be just as concerned as was the Lord with the suffering of the least of the brothers, just as eager to see the reign of poverty and ignorance and suffering come to an end. Chesterton describes this beautifully in the line from *The Ballad of the White Horse* which you have heard me quote so often. He pictures the Mother of God appearing over the banners of King Alfred's army, "Seven Swords were in her heart, but one was in her hand."* When you are teaching your children about the Blessed Mother, Nancy, give them that image instead of the "lovely lady dressed in blue" bit.

Perhaps it might seem that in this and my other letters I am demanding a lot from you. You must wish occasionally that so much was not expected from you, that people would leave you alone, that the harangues from every side would come to an end, that you could just settle down quietly and lead an ordinary life. First of all, I don't think you would be satisfied with an ordinary life. Even more importantly you are not an ordinary person. I wonder if you have ever stopped to think how much work and suffering has been

* Reprinted by permission of Dodd, Mead & Company from *The Ballad of the White Horse* in *The Collected Poems of G. K. Chesterton.* Copyright 1911 by Dodd, Mead & Company.

expended to make Nancy possible. Most of the young people in the Hills have no sense of history, no concrete awareness that life could have been very much different. Parents, of course, tell them about the sacrifices which have been made, but I think young people quickly learn to discount such stories, because they suspect that parents get more satisfaction out of the "benefits" they are able to bestow upon their children than the children do themselves.

Yet your generation represents the pride of a hundred years of effort. You are the hope of the American Church, you are the best that the immigrant groups to the New World have produced. Parents, grandparents, great-grandparents suffered much to make the standard of living you take for granted possible. Priests and sisters have devoted their lives to the creation of the educational system through which you have passed. Young men your age have died in wars defending the freedom which you enjoy. The whole massive American economy and technology is a slave at your feet, ready and eager to provide absolutely anything you want. There are no young people in the world who do not envy your wealth (and wealth it is by any standards the world has ever known) and opportunities. You are part of the privileged one-tenth of one per cent of the human race. No, Nancy, you are not going to be left alone. The world has the right to demand great things of you, to demand that you give it the love and faith it needs, because it has done so much for you. Nor is the Hound of Heaven really going to let you get away, though you have to suffer a great deal before you make that discovery.

I suspect that there may be times when you feel trapped, when actually you are merely called. I don't want to sound like a fatalist, but it is impossible for us to get away from our destiny—impossible in the sense that even though we flee our destiny, it will continue to haunt us. You really are not under any illusions about what your talents are or what you can do with your life. You can, of course, settle for the second-rate. You can deprive the world of the courage and happiness that you would be able to bring it. You can find a bushel and hide under it. But it won't work and deep down you know it won't work. You can pretend that if you are a faithful wife and devoted mother you have discharged your responsibilities; but you know that if you try such an escape, there will always be a quiet voice in the depths of your soul muttering, "Nancy, you've turned your back on life, you're still running away, you're cheating yourself, you're missing something, indeed, you're missing everything." Some people might be able to live with this voice, but you won't be able to and you know you won't.

I am not going to deny that it will take courage to give the world the faith and the love which you can. It would be much, much easier, in the short run, to settle for escape. It always takes courage to be that which we are capable of; and since you are capable of so much, you will be required to display great courage, perhaps more than you can imagine even now. Indeed, if you knew now all the things the Lord is going to demand of you, it is possible that you would never stop running. But, as you must know, happiness is not the absence of difficulty but rather the surmounting of difficulty.

Perhaps the final reason why you should not try to escape that which you can be is that escape will be dreadfully boring.

Enough for now. I guess there will be a big lay mission committee meeting at Easter time, so perhaps I will see you at it, although the Easter vacation is so short, I don't imagine that much will get done.

God bless,

Liturgy and Prayer

Dear Nancy,

The week after Easter is for me one of the most depressing weeks of the year. What depresses me is not the Paschal liturgy which is easily the most lovely of the liturgical cycle, but the fact that Easter Week is ignored by the Christian faithful. All through Lent the churches are filled every day during Mass, the communion rails are crowded, the confessional lines are long. There can be no doubt that Lent is a time of great fervor—at least as far as observable practice goes. But then Easter comes and the fervor is turned off, much as one would turn off the sprinkler on the lawn during the summer time when it has been going too long. So Easter Week, the most important week of the year, the week when we celebrate Christ's triumph over sin and death, is a time of empty churches. People have come to Mass for their Lenten penance; Lent is over and they go back to getting that extra half-hour of sleep. Yet it is true that, if one were to have to choose between going to Mass for the fifty days before Easter and the fifty days after, on theological grounds one would certainly select the latter period.

What depresses me is that we have been telling people this for nine years without the slightest effect. They just don't seem to believe that the Mass is not a penance, but a privilege, that to go to Mass as a Lenten penance is a devotional contradiction, that the celebration of Our Lord's triumph is really more important than its preparation, and that if the Mass really meant something to them, they would not let their good habits go to pieces on Easter Monday morning.

I guess the problem is that we are fighting a superstitious approach to religion which is not defeated merely on the intellectual level. I am not saying that certain practices are superstitious, but that the approach of many people to these practices borders on the superstitious, or at least the compulsive. Thus people know that Mass attendance as Lenten penance is not an appropriate approach to worship, that the purpose of confession is not a detailed listing of the minutiae of sins, that Communion outside of or before Mass is the exception and not the rule, that active participation is the "indispensable source of all true piety," that quality in prayer is more important than quantity, and that sobriety in prayer is more important than unrestrained sentimentality; they know all these things are true, and yet they feel so much more at ease when they are acting the other way that they just keep on doing so.

Thus we have people who orient their prayer life around private devotions, private revelations (and were they surprised when the world survived 1960), private superstitions, and the snack-lunch approach to the Eucharist (the approach which does not see the Eucharist as an integral part of a total act of worship, but rather isolates it from the rest of the Mass). For some reason or other—perhaps because they are expected to pray more in our culture—this kind of spirituality has an especial attraction for girls. Its basically sentimental orientation appeals to the feminine emotionality, especially when that emotionality has never matured. As Fr. H. puts it, it is the "tell your troubles to Jesus" approach to the spiritual life. It tends to be sweet, sticky, groveling, and exaggerated; and its favorite words are "deign" and "vouchsafe."

I don't want to be harsh on the people who are incapable of anything else, but I think it ought to be perfectly obvious that such a spirituality will simply not sustain you through the rigors of the apostolate. The worst thing that could happen to your sacramental life would be that it would deteriorate into a sentimental routine. High school girls tend to flock to church every morning with great determination, either because their Sodality rules demand it or because their grammar school habits survive. Such habitual attendance is all that we can expect from teenagers, but it obviously does not last. Life just becomes too complicated to sustain a regular spiritual life unless it is motivated by something stronger than habit or nunnish approbation. My own feeling is that daily worship is essential to the life of the layman, because he needs the vigor of the sacramental system to be faithful to his Vision and to himself. One grammar school classmate of mine summed it up when he said, "I'd go to hell if I didn't go to Mass every day." He was wrong, of course, but if he had said, "I am not going to be the kind of layman the Lord wants me to be unless I get to Mass as often as I can," he would have been very right. At the Mass we reaffirm our unity with Christ and through Him with our fellowmen. In the Eucharist the triumph of Christ is continued in time and space, and we are made part of that triumph by being given the power to go back to our mission field and by word and life bear witness to the good news of the new life. When it finally dawns on us that without the Mass, we simply cannot do this, then we have at last begun our spiritual growth in the lay vocation.

The liturgy of the Roman rite is also a marvelous restraint on sentimentality; perhaps this is why some people who are nothing but sentiment find it so uncongenial. The prayers and actions of the Mass are so sober and so rational that it is impossible to let ourselves go in an emotional orgy. I am not saying that it is without emotion or without sentiment; all one need do is look at the Easter Vigil to realize that there is plenty of emotion in the Roman liturgy, but it is always a restrained emotion, one that involves us physically since we are not angels, yet forces us to keep our dignity since we are not animals.

The liturgy is not our whole prayer life, yet it must be the center of our prayer and everything else must be to some extent modeled after it. Our contemplation, our private devotions must flow from the liturgy and orient us back towards public worship. We must understand that the official prayer of the Church is public, community prayer; that when we pray publicly we pray not as isolated individuals but as integrated members of the community. Hence when we pray alone we must never try to find isolation in this kind of prayer, we must never try to escape from our obligations to our fellowmen. We pray in solitude, yes, indeed; but we never pray alone since we are members of the Body of Christ.

Some older people find community worship and community responsibility in private prayer very difficult to accept. They were brought up in a day when individualist piety was much more in vogue than it is in our day of liturgical revival. We certainly don't condemn these people, but we also realize that we cannot be like them, that we must flee the temptation to seek out a corner of the church where we can shut out the rest of mankind and communicate with God all by ourselves.

Please don't misunderstand me, Nancy, I am not against contemplation; but as Father Merton's books ought to have established by now, the contemplative is the last one in the world who wants to isolate himself from his fellowmen. His whole purpose in going to a monastery is so that he might love his fellowmen more and serve them better. So you must contemplate. Your vocation may not be that of a contemplative, but you must contemplate. It will never be a contemplation divorced from action and, I fear, never one separated from noise. It will be those moments of contact with the Reality of your Vision which you will find necessary to sustain the operation of the Vision in your life. You will be driven by the needs of your work to contemplate, and the contemplation will drive you back again into the challenge of activity. In the lay life (and in the life of the parish priest, I might add), action and contemplation are inseparable. One dries up without the other.

How does one contemplate? I am not really sure

whether I ought to try to answer that question because I have a hunch that you are probably better at it than I am; indeed, I am amazed at the number of young people of both sexes who seem to have remarkable potentialities for growth in the life of prayer. Some day I will try to figure out the reason for these abilities. Your generation is more sophisticated than mine, has more material possessions, more things to do with its time, and yet for some fantastic reason seems much better at prayer when it chooses to put its mind to it. Few people bother to develop these potentialities and they disappear rather quickly; even at your age they seem to be ebbing and by the middle twenties they are gone. I often wonder what would happen if these abilities were developed in ten or fifteen people. What would a parish do if it suddenly discovered that it had some real mystics within its boundaries? It might prove very embarrassing, especially to the parish clergy. Yet such an event is nothing more than a logical result of the new theology of the laity.

In any event, it seems to me that there are two kinds of contemplation (in addition to reflection about which I think I wrote in another letter), or rather two different sources of material about which we can contemplate. The first kind is scriptural-liturgical and originates from the Bible, either directly through our reading it or indirectly through the reflection of the Bible contained in the liturgy. The second finds its material not from any such formal source but rather from the things and events of every-day life (I presume that the contemplation which results from spiritual reading will be in some fashion connected with the liturgy or the Scripture).

As to the first kind of contemplation, I will not embarrass you by asking you when was the last time that you read the Bible or even read about it. The day is past when Catholics were inclined to believe that they were not supposed to read the Bible—though some Protestants are unaware of this. But now we seem to be in a time when Catholics know that they can read the Bible and in fact should read it, but don't.

Not all parts of the Bible are exactly easy reading (have you ever tried the Book of Numbers, for example?), or of the same value as material for contemplation. However, most of the New Testament does not provide too much difficulty and there are enough good books on the important parts of the Old Testament (*The Two-Edged Sword, A Path Through Genesis, The Seven Books of Wisdom*) to open the riches of these volumes to the layman. The excellent new popular magazine *The Bible Today* should also be a great help. In short, there is just no excuse, other than laziness, for a Catholic layman not steeping himself in the Bible.

In the Scripture God is speaking to us directly, though through a human author. But in addition to this direct revelation there is the indirect revelation of the Almighty through His creatures, through the things that we see and the events we experience in our daily lives. Here once again we may be too busy to notice but God is everywhere—in the beat of the raindrops, the laughter of a child, a street light seen through the trees, the quiet of an early morning, meeting an old friend, helping someone whom we love. It is only when we get old that we fail to see the wonder in life; and there is no reason why we should ever get old as long as we keep our sense of wonder.

152 : LETTERS TO NANCY

In addition to praying, you must do penance—which is nothing more than asserting your mastery over creatures and over yourself. Penance is also called mortification, a form of death; it is only through death that we can come to live and it is only through a partial death to creatures that we begin to live. The world is not evil and neither is the human personality evil. But between the world and the human personality and among the elements of the personality there exists a disharmony which we call Original Sin. Penance is an attempt to reduce the effects of this disharmony to a minimum, to put some order into the disorder that our personality often is, to assert the control of reason over the rest of man.

It may be, Nancy, that a lot of people are engaging in self-denial in our community, but I don't see it. Lent is a time for giving up candy or cigarettes (for a day or two) and getting up to go to Mass. Ember days are a nuisance; fish on Friday a symbol of our faith. But consistent and planned self-restraint—this I think is rare. I would not even know how to suggest where people ought to begin, what kind of worldly pleasures they ought to temporarily set aside. Maybe sometime during the summer we ought to devote a Tuesday night session to this problem. I would be very interested to know what the group thinks on the subject—if they think about it at all.

Let me make clear that privation of some legitimate good is not a desirable thing in itself. We are not puritans and we should make every effort to try not to be Jansenists (though for us Irish it is hard). Self-denial is pursued not as an end in itself but rather as a means of acquiring freedom, for asserting our control over the situation in which we find ourselves, our liberty from the demands of material goods. It is a bit of death which shows that we are able to live even with death and to survive it.

One last thing ought to be said about the spiritual life of the young lay person; there must be in it recollection. You know that our theory calls for formation through action. I don't think there is any question about its validity; the history of things around this parish confirms that no one ever develops zeal by merely talking. Apostolic formation has occurred in the YCS moderators' group at a faster pace than in anything else we have ever done, precisely because people were required to get involved in doing something for others. However, even though formation through action seems to be essential in lay spirituality, action doesn't work by itself. In addition to a bit of reflection or contemplation every day, we must also set aside longer periods of time at intervals in our life to get more perspective and more depth. In the absence of experiences like an annual retreat or several days of recollection a year, I fear that we are going to run out of spiritual energy.

I am not sure that retreats at school are the answer. They serve a purpose but the fact that students are forced to attend them may deprive them of some of their effectiveness. I am not sold on any particular format and by no means persuaded that the traditional kind of retreat is what we are looking for. Our study weeks at the end of the summer are one-third retreat, one-third seminar, and one-third party. I don't really know whether they have any long-range impact, but at least they represent an experiment to learn what kind of "period of reflection" is best suited to the needs of the laity.

But it seems to me to be absolutely essential that there be these "periods of reflection," when you get away for a few days either by yourself or with a few friends for serious thought and discussion and prayer.

I suppose that the format of these "periods of reflection" is just one more problem that we can bequeath to your generation to solve. And, incidentally, why don't people make retreats any more before they get married?

Worship, the sacraments, self-denial, action, contemplation, retreats—these are the essentials of a spirituality for a young lay woman, and, of course, for any Christian. If you don't have these in your life, you will never get out of the minor leagues. I wish, Nancy, that we knew more about the form these things ought to take in the life of people like you, but the honest truth is that we don't; we're just beginning to think about the problems. But I hope that by the time you have daughters in their late teens (and that day will come, almost before you know it) the situation will be very different.

God bless,

The Essential Poverty

Dear Nancy,

Before this long series of letters comes to an end, I think I ought to say something about poverty, since it is such an important part of the Christian life. Like an increasing number of other American Catholics, you have not known the slightest material want since the day you were born. It is possible that, if you make a financially prudent choice for a husband, you never will lack for anything material for the rest of your life. Even if you have to make some sacrifices during the early years of marriage, it is very unlikely that those years will last for long or that they will involve much in the way of privation.

Now I am not saying that such a situation is wrong, or that you and your friends are to be criticized for being free of anxiety about survival or about the comforts of life. On the contrary, physical poverty is not a good thing in itself, but so easily debases the human spirit that the less of it there is in the world the more human the life of man becomes.

Nor do I think that the young people here in the Hills are too dependent on their worldly possessions. It seems to me rather that they are to a remarkable extent indifferent to them. Since they never have had to worry about having such possessions, they do not devote much time and energy thinking about them. The least problem that those who go off to the convent or the seminary seem to have is leaving their wealth behind. The same thing seems to be true of young married couples, when the husband is still in graduate school and the new family is forced to endure what by American standards would certainly be considered poverty. Living in a tiny apartment with battered old furniture and no rugs on the floor seems to strike them as being fun—at least as long as they know it is not going to be permanent.

The problem I have in mind is much more subtle. I suppose it comes to this: what is there left to do for those who have everything—or at least know they can have everything with relative ease? I know one young couple in their early twenties who seem to have everything—two cars, a beautiful big home, new furniture, an established place in the community, and a future which, barring almost impossible disaster, will be completely free from financial problems. They are a wonderful twosome and I think the world of them; but what challenge is left in their life? When you have the American Dream at twenty-five, where do you go next. Or even if it takes till you're forty to achieve the Good Life, then what happens?

The generation that came before us had to work long and hard to become "successful"; they had to struggle through the awful nightmare of the Great Depression, and were able to come to the Hills only with major effort and commitment to their careers. But the struggle for success was sufficient to put considerable meaning and challenge into their lives; whether it was as rewarding as they thought it would be is perhaps another question. But at least it gave them something to fight for. In these days of prosperity and of an expanding upper middle class, your contemporaries will be able to achieve the Good Life with far less effort than was required of your parents. Some of you may not quite reach the heights that your parents have, but you will surely reach a state where you will not lack any of the major comforts you had while you were growing up—and I think that most of you will reach such a state without undue effort and undue excitement.

But after that what happens? If the Good Life, blended with the observance of the Christian Commandments, is the only goal you have, what is there left to do? The trouble with the Good Life as a goal, is that it is not really very satisfying, especially when it comes easy. But if one has decided to settle for economic goals, then the only thing left to do is to seek out more goals of this sort—more money, more possessions, more vacations, more parties and good times. These are not very satisfying either, yet I don't think you are unaware that there are many people who, after a certain stage of life, are really incapable of anything else. The trouble is that, even though you have everything, you will never have enough because no one ever has enough.

So, Nancy, if I may be permitted to use a somewhat unorthodox definition, I would say that for people like you poverty consists essentially in not being satisfied with superficial goals in life, in realizing that such superficial goals in life will never in fact satisfy you. Poverty of spirit is not merely being able to get along without material things; I think you can do this already. It is rather the ability to devote a bare minimum of your concern to such things, because you realize that they are relatively unimportant.

The major mistake you could make would be to put undue emphasis on either the presence or the absence of material goods.

Riches and poverty have no value in themselves. What matters is how we treat them. We have got to use our earthly life to get beyond this earth. We are at work to establish the kingdom of God here as far as we can, which means that the realities of this world must be transfigured, but first we must, so to speak, turn them around. Our point of view is divine, our object is divine, but our material is the realities of this world. It is a carrying-on of the law of the Incarnation. In the same breath Christ states that His Kingdom is not of this world, and claims His rights *in* this world.*

I would think that there are two aspects of this spiritual poverty—a lack of concern about material things and a concern about other things. Spiritual poverty is essentially hope and trust in God. One realizes that one cannot survive without material possessions, that without a certain amount of wealth one cannot play the part of parent and citizen according to one's state in life. One further realizes that he must be

* Pie-Raymond Régamey, O.P., *Poverty* (New York: Sheed and Ward, 1950), p. 18.

prudent and careful, that hope in God does not exclude having a life insurance policy. But the person who has poverty of spirit stops worrying about material things, once he has exercised reasonable foresight. He gives no anxious heed to what he shall eat or what he shall drink or what he shall put on. The important word here is "anxious."

In Father Régamey's words,

What does this teaching mean, . . . first, it urges us to trust in God; secondly—which is really another aspect of the first—it urges us equally strongly not to get ourselves worked up with worries about the future. The second teaching is . . . more important than the first because men tend to combine a theoretical trust in God with great anxiousness over practical matters. The precise meaning of [the Lord's] lesson is not: Let things slide, be like the lilies and the birds and do nothing, but: 'Sufficient unto the day is the evil thereof.' Every day will have its attendant evil, its human suffering. We must be forearmed as far as we can; before we undertake anything, we should sit down and consider what it is possible and sensible for us to do; we should not tempt God. The third truth is a sort of foundation for the two others: God is a good Father. That is why we must trust Him, and our trust must drive out worry. The spirit of poverty makes life so simple, it gets rid of all the fuss that goes with unnecessary worry about the morrow; it is of its nature religious, a loving abandonment of ourselves to our Father.*

The trouble with such a formulation is that while its validity is unarguable in theory, the practical application is often terribly ambiguous. Exactly how much concern, for

* *Ibid.*, pp. 42-43.

example, should parents give to providing for the college education of their children? When does this concern become unbalanced? When does it become anxious? It is perfectly clear that some people allow themselves to go overboard on this subject, to worry about their children's education before they get married, to work themselves into an ulcer or a "nervous breakdown" or a coronary on the pretext that they have to send their children to college. I get a little suspicious about such people and wonder whether the important thing is the education of the children or the fact that the parents have, in the sight of the whole community, sent their children to the best colleges. I often suspect that sending one's children to college is more important for its symbolic value to parents than it is for its education value to children, especially since in our society almost any young person with intelligence and diligence can get through college with only a minimum of parental support. If the concern is really over one's reputation in the community and not over the education of children, then there isn't much doubt about it being anxious. But then if there are no other goals in life beyond "success," and a sign of success is sending your son to Notre Dame (for example), then it is perfectly understandable that you would be anxious about whether you can provide such an education or not. In other words, the measure of your ability to trust in God, after having taken prudent measures of your own, is your ability to live for other goals than the material. We can be detached from worldly possessions precisely to that degree that we are attached to other things.

Thus we pile up treasures in this world for the moth and

the rust to work over, mainly because we have nothing else to do. I have a hunch, Nancy, that for most people greed is merely an attempt to escape from boredom. The young couples we know who are spending money as wildly and as rapidly as they make it, and are eager to make more so they can spend more, are not basically selfish or materialistic; they are just bored; they have nothing else to do and they have to do something. Anxiety about what we should eat and what we should drink and what we should put on merely fills the spiritual vacuum that is to be found in a life that has no other meaning. Nor is it sufficient to say that the "family" can provide the other meaning, because the question is essentially what goals are to be sought for the family.

I am sure, Nancy, that the things I said in the last paragraph are so obvious that no arguments are required to persuade you of their truth. But because they are obvious does not mean that they are easy to apply in practice. Your Vision requires you and enables you to have goals in your life other than the amassing of material goods and pleasures. But you must realize that the vast majority of people with whom you must associate will not have the Vision, and will be unable to look for anything else but the Good Life. The pressures on you to worry about those things about which they worry will be strong. If you are really committed to the work of the Church—which is to say the work of mankind in its most noble manifestation—then you are not going to waste your time with anxious worry about other things. However, commitment comes by degrees and during the next few years of your life you are going to find yourself torn between two

alternatives, and the tension is going to be difficult to resolve
no matter how clearly you realize on the intellectual level
that poverty of spirit is the only way to happiness.

I suppose that this is why it is so important that you and
the man you marry have solid agreement about your attitudes on money and possessions. I suspect that young people
don't talk about these things very much, and that it is only
after they are married that they are in basic disagreement
about the correct orientation towards the things of this
world. In our society such an orientation is so important that
I don't see how a marriage can possibly be happy unless
husband and wife want exactly the same things. Otherwise
their marriage is going to be one long series of bitter arguments about spending. Nothing can so completely destroy
love.

I have talked in this letter, Nancy, mostly about the
spirit of poverty, about that habitual attitude of the personality which keeps it relatively free from anxious concern over
material possessions because it has other and higher values.
However, I don't think that this spirit of detachment can
survive unless it is accompanied by some kind of material
poverty too. By material poverty I don't mean necessarily
giving all that one has to the poor and becoming a beggar,
though I might mean substantially reducing one's standard
of living for a time by working in an organization like the
Peace Corps or PAVLA. The kind of detachment I have in
mind can often (and probably should) be practiced in such
a way that few people would even notice it. One gives up
certain material possessions not because such things are bad,
but because one always wishes to be quite certain that one

is the master of these things and not their slave, that one is
in control of his situation and not controlled by it.

What the problem boils down to is how one can possess anything
at all in such a way as to be oneself possessed by it as little as
may be, and to possess oneself most perfectly. Poverty promises
to set us free and fulfill our innermost being. The problem really
arises only in regard to intelligent beings with free will; only they
can *have*, in the true meaning of the word; only they can possess
anything, because only they can possess themselves. The question
of being and having, then, is bound up with that of freedom,
which is the power of self-possession—the power an intelligent
being has of being the cause of his own action.*

Man makes a major mistake to think that he can *become*
someone by *having* things. Rather the truth is that he is
someone precisely to the extent that he is able to get along
without things, if he has to. He enjoys the goods of this world
to the fullest because he really doesn't need them.

At this point, Nancy, I am sure that you are wishing I
would give some practical examples of what I mean by the
poverty that the young Christian should practice. Here we
run into the same problem that we have encountered so often
before; the practice of the Christian life by the layman is still
an obscure field. Even if the theory is not too clear and few
of us are brave enough to try to say what it ought to mean
in practice, a couple of thoughts do occur to me, although
they hardly represent an organized program of Christian
poverty for the young laywoman. Indeed, I suspect that, if

* *Ibid.*, p. 104.

any such program is to be evolved, it will fall to your generation to produce it.

Let me begin with an area into which a male trespasses
only at considerable risk—clothes. In our society it is expected that women devote considerable concern to the
variety, splendor, and timeliness of their garb—to put things
in as solemn a manner as I can. It would be foolhardy—and
wrong—to say that women should not think about such
things, that serviceable but drab apparel is all they should
wear. Such an injunction would bring down on my head the
wrath not only of most women, but of their menfolk too, and
very properly so. I surely have no objection to women, young
and old, wanting to look their best; indeed, the world would
be a pretty dull place if they did not. However, with all these
cautions and qualifications made, I wonder if I might still
not raise the question as to whether there is not a strong
temptation for girls to devote too much time and energy to
this area of human activity, whether clothes assume an
importance in the lives of many out of all due proportion,
and whether, finally, in some cases the wardrobe does not
become an escape from other and more important forms of
reality. I would not even begin to suggest what due proportion in these matters might be, but will leave this subject—as
so many others—for your generation to work out.

Again it seems to me that many young women of your
age ought to be doing volunteer work during their vacations
instead of working at regular jobs. I know the opposite argument, that even if people do not need to work they still ought
to, so that they might learn the value of money. I find that

this is a highly dubious proposition. I don't think that there are very many people in American society who do not know the value of money, but I think there are a lot of young women who do not know the value of personal charity. It is said that they will get a lot of valuable experience working in an office during the summer months. To which I would reply that there is more valuable experience to be gained by serving Christ in the least of the brothers. I hardly need persuade you of this, Nancy; your summers of such work make your position very clear. But at least you ought to see what you are doing in its proper perspective. You were not running away from responsibility. On the contrary, you were embracing it.

One final practical point—and a very hesitant one at that. I sometimes wonder whether girls expect their dates to spend too much money on them; or rather to put it more specifically, I wonder if they permit their suitors to deceive themselves into thinking that a girl judges admiration and affection in terms of how much a date costs. This is an aspect of human relations about which I know next to nothing, and I will content myself with merely raising the question.

Poverty is a grim subject for everyone but the Christian; I suspect that he is the only one who is so independent of material things that he can laugh at them. If you find, Nancy, that you cannot laugh when you are forced to do without something that you would dearly like to have, then there is an element of attachment in your personality that is going to prevent you from being as happy as you might be.

God bless,

The Cross as Center

Dear Nancy,

May and Spring have come to the Hills. Vacation is near. Fun and good times are presumably to return to our neighborhood. So typically I begin to think I ought to say something about the Cross. Even though you may doubt it still, the theology behind these letters (insofar as they can be said to have a theology) is optimistic. But no optimistic picture is complete if the Cross is left out of it. We inject the thought of the Cross, however, not because it is a shadow which must balance the light of Christian optimism, but rather because it is at the very center of the light.

To begin with, we would make a mistake to look on every pain, every grief, every form of human suffering as the Cross. If such were the case, then we would have to say that the purpose of a cancer research institute would be to remove the Cross from human life, and such clearly would be absurd. The Cross is not blind pain, it is not every obstacle to human happiness. We must be careful that we do not paste the label of the Cross on every kind of suffering. Some obstacles are to be removed from human life; human suffering must go; it is the work of the Christian to keep suffering at an absolute minimum. Fr. H. tells me that the great Italian preacher Father Lombardi was so incensed by the attempt to justify social injustice in the name of the Cross, that he would shout, "The Cross must go!" What he meant, of course, was that the false notion of human suffering, as being a good in itself, had to go. If suffering were a good thing in itself, then the social encyclicals of the Popes, the vast works of charity in which the Church engages, all of these would be not only a waste of time, but positively evil.

The Cross then is not mere pain, but purposeful pain. Suffering is inevitable for man and even though we must do all in our power to reduce it to a minimum, we realize that it cannot be eliminated from the human condition. The function of the Cross then is not to canonize suffering nor to deny its existence, but rather to transform it, to expel the darkness around it, to give it some kind of meaning and purpose. The Cross therefore is not a thing, but an action, a dynamic orientation of the human personality towards suffering which does not over-justify suffering (one's own or others), does not run from it but seeks either to eliminate it or to control it by understanding it. As Fr. H. would put it (and most of these ideas are his) in his best existentialist fashion, the Cross is that dimension of our life by which we are able to absorb the force of evil into our personality and transform it. The Cross may not be a solution to the problem of suffering, but it is at least an obstacle to its perpetuation. It may not be able to change the external situation, but it at least changes the person who is affected by the situation. Indeed, the Cross inclines the Christian to react to evil in precisely the opposite way than that which man normally follows. The ordinary human tendency is to spread our own suffering to others. The Cross, properly understood, helps us to cut short the effects of suffering.

So, Nancy, with this by way of introduction, let's see what it would mean in practice. Let us imagine a situation where two people are unhappily married, where, for example, one of the spouses is an alcoholic. This is undoubtedly evil, it is human suffering of the most difficult kind. Some old-fashioned approaches to the Cross would say that all the other spouse could do would be to put up with the situation, to endure it bravely as a means of getting to heaven. However, there is much more to be said than this. If, indeed, the evil cannot be eliminated it can at least be transformed; it can be absorbed into the personality of the sufferer and changed. It would be so easy for the suffering spouse to let the evil spread by permitting her (or his) own frustrations to be transferred to the children, and thus, as so often happens, give them a very biased picture of marriage, by becoming so miserable and sour that she (or he) would find it necessary to talk to everyone in the community about the faults of the spouse, and thereby spread the evil and unhappiness even farther.

But the Christian would strive to keep the effects of the evil at a minimum, to see that as few lives as possible are touched by it, to absorb into herself (or himself) as much of it as possible so that it will not spread and do even more harm than it is doing. This is demanding heroism, you say?

Well, of course, it is. But if the Cross is to mean anything in the life of the Christian, it must mean heroism. The Christian must do precisely what Christ did with suffering—absorb evil and by so doing transform it into good.

Or again a young widow can go to pieces after the death of her husband (as so many do), becoming a burden to her family and a failure to her children. Thus the evil of death, bad as it is, becomes worse and causes even more harm than it might. If she had been able to rally her emotional resources, she could have at least protected her children from the worst effects of losing their father and by so doing strengthen her own personality and give new meaning to a life which is by no means over.

Or a man dying of cancer can, by his own bravery and faith, protect his family from all the suffering that they might have to endure if he should lose his courage. Even though his pain is acute, his understanding of the Cross enables him to reduce the amount of pain which the situation might cause others.

On a much less serious matter, you know what homesickness can do to people in college and how the homesick and lonely person can spread gloom to a whole residence hall or a whole class. If she had absorbed the loneliness into her own personality and tried to cheer up others, then she would have been able to curtail the depression among her friends. But since she did not understand the meaning of the Cross, she has succeeded in increasing the amount of suffering.

I think the Cross is probably essential to perfecting

human love. In any relationship between two human beings there are bound to be conflicts, disagreements, misunderstandings. All of these things produce pain, hurt, suffering. If two people are really in love they are able to absorb these problems, to prevent them from getting out of proportion, to keep the pain at an absolute minimum. They do this precisely because they do not want the other to be hurt by their own hurt. It is the exact opposite of the situation which one so often sees where hurt is returned for hurt, pain for pain, injury for injury, where love has been replaced by the desire to get even. When the two lovers absorb into their personality the pain that comes from their relationship, they strengthen themselves, they strengthen the relationship, and they thus deepen their love (and at the same time reduce the potential for pain). The Cross turns the lover into a hero and without heroism love is a pretty weak and childish thing.

This approach to the Cross is also essential in the apostolate. The work you will do for the Church is voluntary in the sense that your existence does not depend on it, you will not stop eating or paying the mortgage if you quit. And there are many times as the years go on, Nancy, that you will want to quit. You will find that the work is frustrating, and that your co-workers are often blind and selfish—and sometimes neurotic since the apostolate has a curious attraction for the misfits. You will learn that those you want to help are not interested in being helped, and those who ought to be helping you are too lazy to do so. Unless you can withstand the evil inherent in such problems, the apostolate will be too much for you; you will desert it when the going gets rough or you will engage in petty and bitter factionalism. In either case you will do more harm than good. And I mean that last sentence in the strict sense of the word; instead of reducing the evil in the world as much as lies in your power, you will increase it, you will give the kingdom of darkness more opportunity to contend with the kingdom of light.

The problem with this understanding of the meaning of the Cross is that it runs against a very strong tendency in human nature—the desire to have others carry our cross for us rather than to bear it ourselves. When we are unhappy we rather like to have others unhappy too. When we must suffer it is nice if we know that others are suffering at the same time. The old saying that "misery loves company" is all too true. Indeed it loves company so much that it does all in its power to make others miserable.

The Christian view of suffering is exactly the opposite. If we must suffer we are suffering in order that others might be happy; the dimension which gives meaning to our suffering is that we are trying to protect others from its effects. Thus through a paradoxical aspect of life we are able to find happiness in our suffering because it has become part of love.

Like so many other things you have heard from us, Nancy, all this may sound new and strange. But no matter what you might have heard before, it ought to be clear that this idea of the Cross is so much in harmony with the meaning of the death of the Lord that it must be listened to. What Jesus did by His death was to absorb the evil in the world, to cut its effects, to give meaning to the residual elements that would remain. Jesus did not suffer because suffering was a good thing, but because it was profoundly bad and had to be eliminated. He did not come to lead Christians to seek out suffering because they wanted to be like Him, but rather to destroy suffering because He had begun its destruction. Just as Jesus could only conquer suffering by suffering, so too we can only share in His victory by suffering and at the same time transforming suffering.

I suspect occasionally that our modern piety tends to overlook this element of the Cross, to concentrate so much on pain as to neglect the necessity for its elimination. Such piety, of course, overlooks the lesson of the Good Friday liturgy which does not concentrate so much on grief and sorrow and death as it does on victory. I am not sure that all the misguided emotional overtones of the old *tre ore* services are entirely eliminated from our approach to the Cross.

The Cross is not any longer an instrument of torture but a symbol of triumph. This was clear to those who wrote the liturgy of Holy Week and to those who put the marvelous Byzantine jeweled crosses in their churches. If it is not clear to us, then we really don't understand what Christianity is all about.

There has been much talk about freedom in all these letters—freedom from the marriage mania, from material possessions, from self-deception, from what others want of us. I suppose that all these kinds of freedom are purchased only by suffering, that the Cross is the price of freedom but also its ultimate guarantee. There is no freedom without the Cross, but only the free man (and the free woman) is able to bear the Cross. Unless you are secure in your own selfhood, you will not be strong enough to absorb suffering into your personality; but unless you are strong enough to do that, you have no personality or only the shadow of one which will disintegrate under pressure.

It is not a matter of whether the Cross or selfhood comes first. They both must come simultaneously. Unless you are willing to pay the price of suffering, you will never become yourself, and unless you are brave enough to be yourself, you will not be able to sustain suffering. In fact, you will hardly be strong enough to stay alive.

When you are young, Nancy, I suppose suffering seems rather frightening, something to be ignored whenever possible, something for the old but not for you. Yet even at your age you ought to begin to realize that the light of the Cross is but the setting for the jewel of love.

God bless,

Death or Life

Dear Nancy,

This will surely be the last letter of the current season. One more week and the crew will be home (with the exception of a few world travelers). The Hills will come alive again—at least after a fashion. What opportunities the summer will contain for all of us is known only to the Lord, though I guess the whole of life is like a summer—all kinds of opportunities which sweep by us at such a fantastic rate that we will miss most of them, unless we are always ready to take advantage of the excitement of the present moment.

I should think, Nancy, that this will be an important summer for you, the last one in which you will be a "crazy mixed up" teenager, and perhaps the first one in which your fidelity will begin to look like a liability.

There is no point in denying, Nancy, that the requirements of fidelity are immense. Restraint and care in romantic involvement, professional excellence, intellectual vitality, active charity, prayer, frequent worship—all these are going to require effort, sacrifice, detachment; there is no point in pretending that it is going to be easy. They are not necessary,

175

however, just for fidelity to your Vision. Without them you
are not even going to be happy, you are not going to be
human, you are not going to be yourself. The sacrifices that
fidelity requires are the price you are going to have to pay
for a happy life. As I have told you often before, the Lord
made us to be happy; if we are unhappy it is our own fault.
Unhappiness—which, by the way, is not the same thing as
suffering—is a certain sign that we have lacked the courage
and the determination which it takes to be happy.

One of the things that makes these sacrifices difficult is
that a lot of people are going to tell you that they are absurd.
These are the foes of your Vision, the enemies of your fidelity. They are the nay sayers, the pessimists who were either
afraid to scale the heights or lost their nerve part way up.
They will make fun of you, they will warn you of what you
are missing, will pity your youthful illusions. In the worst
temptation of all they will tell you that you are normal, that
you are no different from everyone else, that you are ordinary
and that you ought to be content with the ordinary happiness
of ordinary life. Instead of "normal" and "ordinary" you
should hear the words "mediocre" and "dull," if you want
to know what they are really saying. They may have your
best interests at heart, they may wish you nothing but well,
but if you listen to them they will destroy you; *and they are
not telling you the truth.* You are not ordinary, Nancy, and
deep down in your heart you know it; whenever you try to
persuade yourself that you are no different from anyone else,
then you are trying to run away. It always seems to stir up
a hornet's nest among young people when I tell them that

they are different, that they are not like other people. They do not like to accept this fact, because of the obligations it implies. So they try to run from the truth and from themselves. In these next months and years the temptation to run from the truth is going to be very strong for you; the temptation to escape from your real self to the carefree, happy-go-lucky front of your phoney self is going to be most seductive. The nay sayers will be urging it on you incessantly. Run you may, but do not think you are going to get away. The Hound of Heaven is after you, Nancy, and He is not going to stop until He catches up with you either to reward your fidelity or to punish your infidelity. (That it will be the former instead of the latter is my hunch, or perhaps only my prayer.) You are not going to escape from Him and there is no point in trying.

Do you ever seriously think that you could be content with being "normal"? Could you possibly believe that your restless spirit could settle down to just an "ordinary" life? Do you think that your conscience would let you have peace if all you could offer to your husband was a wife "just like anyone else"? Would you be able to escape strong guilt feelings if you cheated your future children out of the very extraordinary kind of mother that you are clearly capable of being? And what about the Lord who has guided the human race through hundreds of thousands of years of history to the point where it is able to produce a handful of people like you? When He reviews all the gifts He has showered on you, gifts which certainly put you in the upper one hundredth of one per cent of young women who ever lived, do you seriously believe that He will accept in return a "normal" life and the plea, "I was not any different from the rest"?

Your values may be hard for your family to understand. Like all of our parents they grew up in a very different world, and they find the problems and the concerns and the fears of the contemporary age very difficult to understand. Yet I think most parents in the long run are willing to respect the integrity of their children if the authentic nature of this integrity is made clear. They may not go for posing or for fads or for temporary enthusiasms, but when they encounter something that is rooted in the depths of the personality of their children, they admire it even if they are unable to comprehend it. The older generation met its challenges bravely and well; they kept the faith during the trying years of immigration, Depression, and war. They may find it hard to fathom the fact that the younger generation has its own challenges, but they cannot help be impressed when young people seriously try to meet these challenges. This does not mean that there will not be conflict, because conflict is part of growth towards maturity; but it does mean that the conflict can be understood and expected to be only temporary.

Many of your own generation will bitterly attack your fidelity, at least some of them because if you are right then they are wrong, if your Vision is valid, then they are wasting their lives. As the Scripture says, "Let the dead bury their dead." These people are so often walking corpses, they have become old men and old women while still in their very early twenties. I hate most wedding receptions, Nancy (though this will not excuse you from inviting me to yours), for about the same reason I do not like wakes; the living do not like to be around the dead. I do not mean the bride and groom are dead—though they may be in the act of committing spiritual suicide—but so many of the so-called younger people who gather for the ritual conversations at the reception are very dead. They have lost their Vision, they have killed their fidelity and in the process they have killed themselves. What disturbs me is that I knew them when they were alive, during those few short months or years when they could have been different, when they had a bright and splendid opportunity to be human.

There are another set of enemies to your fidelity that I must mention—the clergy and the religious, and not merely because an occasional one of them will write you a long and tedious letter. You are a threat to us really, because the dedicated layman makes us realize how poorly we have kept our own Vision. We will try to persuade you that you must be a nun. There is such a terrible shortage, you see, and besides we can produce all kinds of proof that the religious state is the more perfect state (which it is in theory and in practice for those who are called to it). We will imply that there is not really very much for you to do in the world except to raise a good family. We will urge you to believe that if you are a good mother that is all that counts. (What wild nonsense! The world is filled with "good mothers" in the sense the words are ordinarily used, and social injustice, oppression, tyranny, suffering and hunger continue unabated.) We will be suspicious of your zeal and skeptical of your enthusiasm. We will urge you to settle down and have a large family and please do not bother us, save perhaps to run a card party or to contribute to an alumnae drive. Or perhaps worse, we will try to persuade you that our own particular brand of the apostolate is the only one that you should be interested in, the only one that suits your talents. When we begin to speak this kind of foolishness, do not listen to us.

I would not leave you thinking, Nancy, that you are going to have to fight these battles for fidelity alone. Eventually you will, I presume, fight them together with a husband whose ideals are the same as yours. But even before then, there are all kinds of girls your age who feel as you do, whose Vision is the same as that of your better self—your "non-normal" real self. They often remain silent because they are afraid to speak or because their background has not even provided them with a vocabulary to articulate their feelings. You are for weal or woe a leader. You inevitably attract followers (and I suppose just as inevitably opponents, such is the price of leadership); you will either lead a large number of people to the heights or the depths. There may be times when you may not like the idea but all kinds of your friends depend on you; and to tell the truth you depend on them. If you display the kind of insight and vigor of which you are capable, they will provide a climate of courage and fidelity that will sustain you in your more depressed moments. On the other hand, if you fail them, they will not be there to help you when you need help.

These are great days to be alive, Nancy; perhaps the

most exciting days since the time when the Church first tentatively began to probe the possibilities outside of Jerusalem. Pope John has thrown open the window and the warm winds of spring are blowing after a long and cold winter. To paraphrase Winston Churchill, no matter how long the Catholic Church lasts, its members will look back on these times and say that this was truly one of our finest hours. You can be a part of all this; you can be involved in one of the great turning points in history. You are free not to, of course; you can turn your back, but I should think that it would be rather hard if you really understand what is going on in the Church today. There must have been many times when you thought that the odd things you were hearing at the Rectory about Catholic Action and the Liturgy and the Ecumenical Movement were the crackpot notions of a handful of disturbed clergymen. In these days after the Second Vatican, we all know better; we are riding the wave of the future. Our side has won.

Well, Nancy, the sermonizing comes to an end. There is much more that ought to be said, but there is just so much that words can say. God has given you the beginnings of life, just one life, but one whole life to do with, in the final analysis, as you wish. He has put into your care someone very wonderful—the person you are capable of being. You are now, by the grace of God, the beginnings of someone wonderful, but only the beginnings; what you do with those beginnings is entirely up to you. You can kill off the Nancy that God wanted you to be, you can prevent her from ever having a chance, you can crush her before she even begins to work the good of which she is capable and to which she is called. You can settle for some kind of second-rate Nancy that God will, of course, love, but in which He will be very disappointed; if you commit this ultimate infidelity, I have no doubt that you will save your soul, but you will go through life hating yourself. The Nancy that God wants to be is a pretty strong customer; and you are not going to stamp her out without a fight, and if you do, I fear that she will come back to haunt you. As to the "ordinary" Nancy who would settle for something mediocre, in the words of the Lord High Excutioner in *The Mikado,* "she never will be missed, no, she never will be missed."

Enough. There is just so much your friends can do for you or say to you. Your decisions or series of decisions in the next few months are going to have to be made alone—in the chill loneliness that each soul must endure when it is locked with its God in the awful moments when its destiny is determined. Your own restless temperament which makes your longings for the Absolute more powerful will both drive you to a decision and make the decision more agonizing. During these moments there is very little we can do; watch, wait, if needs be, listen, pray. What will happen? None of us knows for sure, but, appearances to the contrary, I am an incurable optimist.

God bless,